# LIVE THE LIFE YOU DESERVE

# LIVE THE LIFE YOU DESERVE

## HOW TO LET GO OF WHAT NO LONGER SERVES YOU AND EMBODY YOUR HIGHEST SELF

## SYLVESTER McNUTT III

**HAY HOUSE LLC**
Carlsbad, California • New York City
London • Sydney • New Delhi

Copyright © 2024 by Sylvester McNutt III

**Published in the United States by:** Hay House LLC: www.hayhouse.
com° • **Published in Australia by:** Hay House Australia Publishing Pty
Ltd: www.hayhouse.com.au • **Published in the United Kingdom by:** Hay
House UK Ltd: www.hayhouse.co.uk • **Published in India by:** Hay House
Publishers (India) Pvt Ltd: www.hayhouse.co.in

*Cover design:* Milan Bozic  • *Interior design:* Karim J. Garcia
Illustration on page 105 used under license from Shutterstock.com

**Cataloging-in-Publication Data is on file at the Library of Congress**

**Hardcover ISBN:** 978-1-4019-7615-6
**E-book ISBN:** 978-1-4019-7616-3
**Audiobook ISBN:** 978-1-4019-7617-0

10  9  8  7  6  5  4  3  2  1
1st edition, August 2024

Printed in the United States of America

SUSTAINABLE
FORESTRY
INITIATIVE

Certified Chain of Custody
Promoting Sustainable Forestry

www.forests.org
SFI-01268

SFI label applies to the text stock

*I dedicate this book to you, the reader.*
*Without you, this work would be meaningless.*

# CONTENTS

# INTRODUCTION

One of the top five wishes of the dying is that they had more time. More time to love and live, to wander and dream, to laugh and experience the ones they came to know through life. More time to play, to sing, to dance. More time to float and think. More time to get clear on what they want, need, and crave. The dying wish for more time with their loved ones, kids, or parents. I believe with all my soul that we should not wait until we are dying to start living. Through my years as a coach, friend, father, author, I've learned that everything we value and crave often requires a commitment, a curiosity, and a level of competence in order to unlock the next level. The problem that we are faced with, however, is our limited mindset, our traumas and pain, and the external forces of society.

I believe in exploring the human experience with imagination, curiosity, and a thirst for deeper expansion. I'm not afraid to speak about my realizations and learning, and I love giving credit to moments that inspire me to think and feel. There are mystical aspects of human existence and deeper levels of consciousness that require processes for you to tap into them, and we're going to explore them in this book. My hope is that this serves you on a soul level. I hope this book teaches you, reminds you, or brings something out of you. I've coached thousands of people and helped them get results that have been life-changing.

I plan to offer you the same value as the people who get on calls with me every week.

I write to you in a conversational tone, imagining us as two friends having a warm cup of coffee together on a cool fall day, exploring ideas and feelings with one another. I am here for you. I am your coach, your advocate, and your friend. I want you to sit with me at our coffee table as we dive through the rabbit hole of what it means to live the life we deserve. This book acts as our safe space with each other, where every type of conversation can be had without judgment and where laughter and support can ensue. I believe in judgment-free friendships and open relationships—yes, open to expansion, to love, to healing and being a refuge for one another, and to getting to know the person's soul over and over.

I feel called to serve, and I imagine that you too are a servant, a lover, and a giver. I wrote this book with a great deal of love inside of me, and I hope you can feel the love and passion. I am not here to be right or perfect; I am here as a vessel to serve my gift of writing with the hope that it will help us go deeper into our own expansion. And if we can go one layer deeper, I hope that we can serve our kids, partners, friends, and communities better.

As stewards of the earth, we owe it to our ancestors to learn from them and advance what they gave us while still honoring their journeys through the expansion of our eras. As the creators of life, we owe it to our children and those who will come after us to learn, to chase the highest knowledge, and to heal the deepest wounds so we can live the life we deserve. We cannot show the children of this earth the path of success, enlightenment, and joy if we do not live there ourselves. Children are sponges. They soak up the energy of those around them.

Yes, I struggle, and I have hard days. There are things that I wish I could change as well. But mostly, I feel lucky, advantaged, and blessed in this moment with all the gifts that have been given to me and the opportunities that have found me. My only mission is to share the gold, the love, the ideas. This mission is my life's purpose, and I thank you for being here on this journey with me.

I have a big ask of you on this journey. I want you to journal every day or as often as possible for at least 10 minutes—this single habit has saved and changed my life. As you read this book, you will find journal prompts based on the content. But feel free to ignore those and simply set pen to paper, writing intuitively. Journaling is a tool that helps you go deeper; it helps you process what you think and feel, and it helps you arrive at a zone of expansion. Yes, I am the guide, but this is *your* work and *your* journey.

I have written everything I could in this book to help you *live the life you deserve*, but that's simply an entry point. Once you integrate the lessons and teachings and, most importantly, allow your consciousness to be expanded by the work, then we as friends can see that we have impacted the world.

*Let us choose our medicine so that we may*
*serve, give, heal, and love at our highest levels.*

As stewards of the earth, we owe it to our ancestors to learn from them and advance what they gave us while still honoring their journeys through the expansion of our eras. As the creators of life, we owe it to our children and all those who will come after us to learn, to chase the highest knowledge, and to heal the deepest wounds so we can live the life we deserve. We cannot show the children of this earth the path of success, enlightenment, and joy if we do not live there ourselves. Children are sponges. They soak up the energy of those around them.

— **Sylvester McNutt III,** *Live the Life You Deserve*

CHAPTER 1

# SEEING YOURSELF AS YOUR HIGHEST SELF

The first step to living the life you deserve is to see yourself as your highest self. This requires you to confront limiting beliefs, to let them go, and to create a new personal reality. The way you see yourself shapes your behavior. Your behavior creates your lived outcomes. Your lived outcomes create your experienced emotions. Your interpretation of your emotions is your human experience.

To become one with the life you want to live, let's start at the beginning: examining your self-image.

If you genuinely consider what kind of life you want and get serious about what you want, you 100 percent can create it.

— **Sylvester McNutt III,** *Live the Life You Deserve*

Your highest self is a form of you that sees it all and accepts it all with loving kindness. Your highest self is the version of you that accepts, without judgment, who you are. Your highest self is you in your wholeness, living in reality—understanding cause and effect, consequences, and how to commit to a journey.

— **Sylvester McNutt III,** *Live the Life You Deserve*

When I was 12 years old, my father pulled a gun on me. It all started with him calling me into his room in the back of our apartment in Palatine, Illinois.

"Yes, Father?"

"Close your eyes," he said.

I obeyed. I stood in front of him, eyes shut, as he sat at the edge of his waterbed that was nestled in a wooden box frame. He was wearing a dingy tank top and had a curly afro. A black boombox sat at the back of the room, blasting sounds into the atmosphere. The air smelled like Jack Daniel's and Newport 100s, but the space was clean and organized.

"Open your eyes."

I opened my eyes to one of the many guns that my father owned directly in front of my face. My $20/20$ vision was split and blurred, and the object became two as my eyes adjusted.

"When I tell you to do something, you do it right away. You don't give me attitude and you don't talk back to me—you just do it. Do you understand?"

I shifted my blurred gaze from the barrel of his gun so I could look him in the eye. I could see that he didn't have an evil or malicious intent.

"Yes, sir. I understand."

"You won't be living in this house much longer. What do you want to do when you get out into the real world? What type of life do you want to live? What type of life are you going to create for yourself?" he asked.

"I want to play in the National Football League as a running back for the Chicago Bears, and I want to write books that inspire people. I want to travel around the world and eat different food."

"NFL? Okay, you can do that." My father affirmed my dream with zero doubt in his voice. "Write books, interesting. Well, whatever you want to do, you need to work harder than everyone else. You need to be your highest self. To do that, you need to see yourself as your highest self every single day.

"That is why I am so hard on you. You like to play too much. You need to focus, work, and stay dedicated to your dreams. You need to study, you need to train, and you need to be the best. Get the fuck out of my room and go get started. Don't miss any more of your chores—you're a McNutt. We require excellence in this house."

Even with a gun in my face, there was no fear or worry. I simply replied, "Yes, sir," and left the room. Yes, I know that was a traumatic thing—no person should ever have to worry about such threats from a loved one. But I was used to my father using unnecessary and overly dramatic behaviors to prove a point or to make me think. I believe my father was one of the smartest people who ever walked the face of the earth; he just didn't present his teaching in a safe way.

My father grew up with hard work and dedication instilled in him from his parents. Order, cleanliness, and self-discipline were further ingrained in him due to his years serving in the U.S. Army. At the time, he was upset that I didn't clean and do my chores in a timely manner based on his often unrealistic and controlling perspective. He saw it as a lack of discipline, something he harped on every single day. These extreme tactics were needed, he thought, to ensure that a lack of discipline in one area of my life wouldn't spread to influence *every* area of my life.

This story is when my father gave me access to the first key to living the life you deserve: "What do you want to do with your life?" That simple question, if taken seriously, can paint an image and direction for us, no matter who we are, no matter where we are.

I went back to the room that I shared with my sister and thought about what it would mean to live on my own, to take care of myself, to go after those dreams that I told my father about. My parents had just bought me a new journal earlier that week, so I fetched it from the top of the closet where I'd placed it. I grabbed a pen and wrote a big and bold title on the cover, my father's voice resonating in my head: **Highest Self.**

I lay on the bottom bunk bed and drifted into the dream space of *what could be.* I closed my eyes as emotions and thoughts ran through me. Even though I was daydreaming into the future, it felt like the experience of déjà vu. I vividly saw myself celebrating a touchdown on the football field, my arms up in the air, thousands of people chanting and cheering for my team. I saw myself writing in the jungle of Costa Rica. I saw myself riding bikes and feeling the crisp mountain air in my lungs. I saw myself as an older version: good-looking, magnetic smile, and stylish hair. I saw myself smiling and enjoying life. I saw a happy version of me. I saw joy.

Over the next decade, I documented everything. I journaled daily, completely filling up my "highest self" journal and several more. While I didn't play for the Chicago Bears, I was able to actualize my dream of football success. I played in high school at one of the most prestigious schools in the country, and then I walked on to a Division 1 football team at Northern Illinois University. (For those unfamiliar: Division 1 is the highest level of competition, achieved by only 1 to 3 percent of high school football players. "Walking on" means that I was not recruited by that team and instead had to hustle hard, network, and prove my worth for my spot.) After two years of college football, my dreams kept calling. I spent two more seasons playing professional arena football before I retired. At the end of my football journey, I felt complete closure and happiness. I didn't reach the exact goal that I came up with as a kid, but the actual experience was perfect for me.

During that same time, I was committed to understanding the magic of language. I knew I wanted to be an author because I was always a great storyteller, whether it was at parties, with girls I liked, or with younger kids who could never stay focused. I leaned in to storytelling to connect to another's soul, as a way to seize people's time and attention while leaving them with encouragement or empowerment.

In 2010, a couple years after the end of my football career, I was at a poetry open mic show in Chicago, Illinois. Standing onstage in front of 500 people, I was shaking inside, but on the outside I was as calm as a Buddhist monk in the middle of a meditation session. I felt I'd been prepared for this by the high-pressure situations of playing football in front of thousands, with coaches and crowds screaming. I felt thankful for the misguided "tough love" lessons of my father because no heckling could compare to that. I knew I was destined to speak, teach, and lead.

I'll never forget the feeling of standing in front of the crowd and saying that first line of my poem—it felt like home.

*"You only get one life to become your highest self."*

I went on for another 20 lines or so, but it felt like I was up there for days. "Time and Self" was a poem that took me about three years to perfect. When I was finished, the audience was moved to clap, and it was more than the performative okay-thank-you-for-coming participation clap. We've all experienced that type of clap, and I'm not here to knock it because at times, we need that. This was a vibrant one; you could feel people clapping with their soul.

That open mic poetry night in Chicago was one of my most important human days. I knew I was meant to write, but I didn't have validation from the outside world until that moment. Eventually, my writing career took off, and I started selling books—lots of them—all over the world. For the past 15 years, I have been a full-time author, committing myself to the art of tangling words and learning about psychology, spirituality, meditation, journaling, communication models, neuroscience, and how to be a human in this ever-changing world.

I never imagined myself as a coach, but suddenly people started reaching out, begging me to guide them, to show them a way out of suffering and into alignment with their highest self. And so, for the last decade, I have also been a self-mastery coach.

My father was able to witness some of my football success but died before getting to see my success as a writer, a coach, and a parent. He didn't get to see the dedication that went into this. He didn't get to see the pain and tears that I've shed over this magic.

Now that I have the luxury of seeing how this plays out, I can say with 100 percent certainty that my father was right about the key he gave me on that one traumatic/ enlightening day:

> *If you genuinely consider what kind of life you want*
> *and get serious about what you want,*
> *you 100 percent can create it.*

Having a clear vision of what you want is the most important north star in life. Go for a long walk; think and feel into it. What do you want? How do you want to live? If you get clear on those questions, life will support you and conspire to give you a reality close to your vision.

We're all working with different definitions of what our highest self looks like. Some people might see the term and think it's just a woo-woo spiritual phrase. My father had his understanding, and my own has changed from when I first started writing in my journal to now. So I'd like to leave you with one of the definitions I meditated on recently, then I'd like you to come up with your own.

## WHAT IS *YOUR* HIGHEST SELF?

July 2022. I was in San Diego, California, for a month, taking my first yoga teacher training program. I studied at the prestigious Trilogy Sanctuary under the leadership of Gabrielle Blachley, whose energy is powerful to the soul like the echoes of a symphony. Imagine taking a class in the most serene place, on a building rooftop under an airy white geodesic dome, with a view of the Pacific Ocean. You could lean on the edge of the bricks and peer at the waves at any moment.

One of the questions she asked us during class stayed with me forever, and I am going to leave you with the same question to journal on. Even if you love my answer and my response is sufficient, it's important that you come to your own conclusion for your journey.

At first, I cringed when she asked this. I despise anything that feels too woo-woo, and come on. San Diego vibes. Ocean. Yoga. I'm thankful I left my judgmental analytical brain and just did the assignment because that journal session prompted some deep thought that I didn't know I needed.

The question: What is your highest self?

In my journal, I wrote:

*Your highest self is the most authentic version of who you are in this moment. The society we live in does a great job of inviting us to live in fear-like consciousness, under the cloud of perfectionism, and we become addicted to wearing masks and cloaks that hide who we truly are. Society has given us distraction after distraction to keep us hiding and has created drugs to make us run from our emotions, from our problems, from our quirky personality traits. Your highest self is a form of you that sees it all and accepts it all with loving kindness. Your highest self is the version of you that accepts, without judgment, who you are. Your highest self is you in your wholeness, living in reality—understanding cause and effect, consequences, and how to commit to a journey.*

*It's possible that we may not know our highest self until a transformation occurs. That transformation can be the abolishment of alcohol or other drugs. It can be a total acceptance of accountability or even the completion of a particular study or educational program. It's possible that learning who you are and living in the energy of your highest self will happen once you move out from under your parents. That's when an entirely new level of life occurs.*

*Your highest self is who you are when you are not grading yourself, when you are not trying to be perfect, when you are connected to the highest consciousness that you can achieve based on your body, your brain, your life. Reaching your highest self means ridding yourself of any excuses, any of the stories that keep you stuck in yesterday. It means that you are in total alignment with the lived outcomes you want.*

*Your highest self is who you are when you focus on what keeps you nourished, what heals you, and what gives you a higher quality of life. Your highest self is the version of you that is real and authentic, the version of you that goes for the desires you seek. You are responsible and allow joy and love to be a big part of your life.*

Pause now to reflect in your journal: What is your highest self?

## REVEAL YOUR MIND TRAPS TO DISCOVER YOUR HIGHEST SELF

For you to become your highest self, we need to free your mind.

To free your mind, we need to understand your mind.

Stop guilt.

Stop blaming.

Stop beating yourself up.

Stop—this is a journey as two explorers to observe, not to judge.

There are certain mindsets and actions that will help you get into alignment with your highest self and the life you want to live. And there are some mindsets and actions (*schemas*) that keep you trapped, that ruin you, that keep you in the darkness. In psychology, the word *schema* refers to mind traps that may hold us back. These are broad, pervasive themes that shape our self-perception and interactions with others.[1]

When the fundamental emotional needs of a child remain unfulfilled, schemas emerge. They evolve throughout our lifetime, forming the basis for destructive patterns. When we observe our own negative or self-sabotaging behaviors, in some cases we are observing our inner child behaving in a particular way as an adult in the hopes that we will be seen and loved.

Maybe you see yourself in some of these schemas, and this becomes the catalyst you need to break away. I invite you to bring light, attention, and energy to the wound that caused your schema. Then change the language of your story and the depth of your values.

Give yourself the compassion you need to grow into a new mental model. Understand that if you've had the same thought patterns for 10, 20, or even more years, a change won't happen right away. It takes repetition and time to rewire the brain. (In neuroscience, this is called *neuroplasticity*.) If I met you at the park with a football every single day and taught you how to throw a spiral, then no matter where you currently are in that journey, you'll eventually be able to throw a spiral better than 99.9 percent of the population. Why? Because your value system changes through repetition. Before, you didn't value throwing a spiral. Now, you've met me at the park every day—clearly your value system has changed. This is neuroplasticity in action.

In this way, we use neuroplasticity to rewire our brains and create the life we deserve.

# COMMON PSYCHOLOGICAL SCHEMAS[2]

### 1. Emotional Deprivation

The belief and expectation that your essential needs will never be satisfied. It entails a sense of lacking nurturing, care, guidance, protection, and empathy from others.

### 2. Abandonment

The belief and expectation that others will leave, people are unreliable, relationships are fragile, loss is inevitable, and you will ultimately end up alone.

### 3. Mistrust/Abuse

The belief that others are inclined to be abusive, manipulative, selfish, or intent on harming or exploiting you. Trust becomes a challenging prospect.

### 4. Defectiveness

The belief that you are flawed, damaged, or unlovable. This leads to the anticipation of rejection from others.

### 5. Social Isolation

A prevailing sense of loneliness and alienation, feeling detached and separate from others.

### 6. Vulnerability

The perception of the world as a perilous place, with the constant threat of catastrophe and feeling overwhelmed by forthcoming challenges.

### 7. Dependence/Incompetence

The belief in your inability to make effective decisions so you must rely on others' judgment for everyday responsibilities.

### 8. Enmeshment/Undeveloped Self

The feeling of lacking an independent identity separate from family, partners, an authority figure, and so on.

### 9. Failure

The expectation of personal failure or the belief that you cannot perform well enough.

## 10. Subjugation

The conviction that you must submit to the control of others lest you face punishment or rejection.

## 11. Self-Sacrifice

The belief that sacrificing your own needs excessively for the sake of others is necessary.

## 12. Approval-Seeking/Recognition-Seeking

The perception that gaining approval, attention, and recognition outweighs authentic self-expression and staying true to yourself.

## 13. Emotional Inhibition

The conviction is that you must restrain self-expression to avoid rejection or criticism from others.

## 14. Negativity/Pessimism

The pervasive belief that the negative aspects of life outweigh the positive ones. This is accompanied by pessimistic expectations for the future.

## 15. Unrelenting Standards

The belief that one must always strive for perfection or avoid making mistakes to meet impossibly high standards.

## 16. Punitiveness

The belief that you (and others) should be harshly punished for errors or shortcomings.

## 17. Entitlement/Grandiosity

The sense of being special or superior to others, disregarding rules and potentially causing harm. This is often driven by a desire for power or control.

## 18. Insufficient Self-Control/Self-Discipline

The perception of being incapable of accomplishing goals, particularly when faced with tedious, repetitive, or frustrating tasks. It also involves succumbing to impulsive behaviors with detrimental consequences.

## HOW TO GET OVER YOUR MENTAL BLOCKS STEP-BY-STEP

In order to get to your next level tomorrow, you must release the mental traps of today and yesterday. Forgive yourself for your mistakes and for what you didn't do well. Focus on your gifts, what is working in your favor, and the endless possibility that exists around each one of us. You are more powerful than you've been giving yourself credit for. Think big about what you can do. Feel the love and compassion in your heart and focus on what you can control each day. If you free your mind from negativity and the past, you have more energy for the moment and for being a conscious creator of your future.

When I first met my client Jasmine, she had a mentality and self-identity that was soul-crushing. She was stuck in this loop: Don't express yourself because of the fear that you are flawed. Hide from opportunity because you fear being seen. Even when smart enough or good enough, you must hide and cower due to the belief that you are flawed.

I was able to recognize two major schemas: emotional inhibition and defectiveness. Because this mental model was such a large part of Jasmine's identity, she felt trapped. That's when she hired me. I work with "trapped" people all the time. When we say things like "I am trapped," we are talking about the conflict of our inner knowing versus the habit that we have had for years. There is a war inside between the scared, unloved inner child and our highest self trying to come out.

The voice of your highest self is trying to communicate with you, but your schemas do not want to hear it—and both are fighting to be the main player in your story. That's why you feel trapped. Even if you don't have these mind traps, this is what they all do: they trap us in this story, in these emotions, in this landfill of no imagination or possibilities.

We are not trapped; we just *feel* trapped. So what do we do?

1. *Identify the mental block and take full ownership of it.* Not blame, but ownership. Blame is the emotion of guilt; ownership puts you into the energy of a leader. An empowered mind can create experiences far beyond what a disempowered mind can comprehend.

2. *Make a commitment to let go and mute your mental block.* It's most effective if you focus on one mental block at a time. Focus on one thing at a time for a set period. Nothing happens until you make this first commitment to change your value system from that of the schema to that of your highest self.

3. *Shed light on the rest of your story.* Healing means wholeness. When we talk about what we can't do, how we messed up, or where we fall short, we rarely mention our gifts of strength. Yes, you messed up, you have flaws, *and* you have evidence in your life of greatness, of miracle, of success. Start telling your story in full and not just the dark, shameful, flawed parts.

4. *Set healthy boundaries.* Leave the environments that reinforce the lowest versions of you. Set boundaries around people who talk negatively or put limitations into your

dreams—including you. We no longer have time for that.

5. *Stay committed because repetition rewires the brain.* You need to stay on the mission in order for it to be completed. This will be hard, and it will be worth it. You will change any limiting beliefs, but it takes time, effort, and compassion—all of which I know you have because you are reading these words today. You are not out of time. You're reading a book that is telling you that you're capable of more and that compassion is central to all human beings.

The mental blocks that Jasmine had were reinforced by her language, so our priority was inserting some new language. Instead of speaking about and focusing on what would go wrong, she needed to bring her focus to what was going well and what was possible. She was creating from a wound and a source of lack, so I asked her what it would look like to create and move from a place of abundance. Little mental shifts like this become massive waves, but you can't just do it once and be done. You need repetition here.

Getting over mental blocks is a process. I wish it were as easy as identifying them and then flipping a switch! Instead, these shifts are made over and over. I would ask Jasmine at the top of each of our calls, "What is your highest self communicating to you?" As her coach, I didn't want to feed her any answers; I wanted her to determine them for herself. I would just hold the frame, hold the space, and hold the confidence for her to borrow so she could find it on her own.

In time, Jasmine began to set healthy boundaries with people who reinforced scarcity, lack, and negativity. As a consequence, her energy went to a higher level. Each call was a portal for her to be reminded of all that was going well and in her favor. After our sessions ended, I was happy to see her move forward with a new mindset and new energy, living in alignment with her highest self.

If you do not have a coach, one of the best ways you can reinforce your new mindset is to journal. I recommend describing the exact mindset you want and revisiting it daily. Journal about your wins, all the possibilities you see, and the things you feel gratitude for. The repetition of writing specific positive thoughts can only give you benefits. It can only give your clarity and remind you of your highest self.

# JOURNAL PROMPTS:
# GO DEEPER INTO UNDERSTANDING THE HIGHEST SELF

Writing will unlock a new layer of thought and feeling. Writing will help you get clearer on what you think, how you express yourself, and how you show up.

Do not skip this. Get your journal out and write.

- While imagining your highest self, **envision** the person you aspire to be in all aspects of life. What values does this version of you hold sacred?

- What dreams and passions lie dormant within you, waiting to be awakened?

- We each have **self-imposed limitations** and boundaries on our potential. Name your limiting beliefs and ponder if holding on to them is necessary. What beliefs, habits, or fears prevent you from realizing your highest potential?

- Contemplate the interplay between **self-acceptance** and self-improvement. How can you embrace and honor your current self while striving to become your highest self? Explore the delicate balance between contentment and the pursuit of personal evolution.

- Imagine your highest self as a source of unwavering **compassion and love**. How can you extend this boundless kindness to yourself?

Fall in love with the possibilities of who you can become. Fall in love with the journey of accepting who you have been. Fall in love with the fact that you have the choice each day to design the life you want, to step into the energy that is your highest self. Fall in love with the option to release the idea of playing small. You were not put here to fit into perfect boxes and ideals. Fall in love with the journey of becoming your highest self.

— **Sylvester McNutt III,** *Live the Life You Deserve*

Free your mind from impostor syndrome. You are more than capable of living the life and having the experiences you imagine. Step 1: Don't compare yourself to another person. Step 2: Go within and get clear on what you want. Step 3: When you get clear on what you want, commit and never look back.

— **Sylvester McNutt III,** *Live the Life You Deserve*

I need more people to understand this: wealth is not about intelligence but how you view yourself. The relationship cycles we enter are not about looks but how you view yourself. The happiness you feel is about how you view yourself, your story, and what is possible in your life. Choose to see yourself as your highest self. Live as an embodiment of that version and release what is beneath you.

— **Sylvester McNutt III,** *Live the Life You Deserve*

Having a clear vision of what you want is the most important north star in life. Go for a long walk; think and feel into it. What do you want? How do you want to live? If you get clear on those questions, life will support you and conspire to give you a reality close to your vision.

— **Sylvester McNutt III,** *Live the Life You Deserve*

## CHAPTER 2

# THE BIGGEST SECRET TO 10X YOUR LIFE

No matter where you are in life, a secret power is always available to you. From your youth, you know what this trick is. You used it repeatedly as a child, but as you grew up, the world extracted a certain seriousness out of you. This seriousness has caused you to forget the power of this ability. It costs no money and no time and gives you more energy and life. You can access this ability today and every day thereafter.

L ife is fragile, and there is an invitation for you to honor what you hold sacred and for you to use your beautiful mind so it can conjure up situations and outcomes that serve you on the highest levels.

— **Sylvester McNutt III,** *Live the Life You Deserve*

S ome of the most remarkable experiences and transformations come from having the audacity to say yes. Say yes, and say it with a smile. Allow yourself to feel worthy of the life you are creating, and live your life to the fullest.

— **Sylvester McNutt III,** *Live the Life You Deserve*

## YOUR IMAGINATION IS THE SECRET

Imagination is an astonishing faculty of the human mind, a way of bringing forth something that doesn't currently exist in reality. Imagination gives you the license to design your life, to see your way out of darkness, to be an alchemist and create what is not present. Imagination is the path to wealth if you are from poverty. Imagination is the way you improve your athletic performance if you feel weak and fragile. Your imagination is an access point to a portal that will take you through and beyond any struggle. You can become who you want to become—you have permission to play and be the creator of your majestic life. You have permission to declare a new reality, a new way of living, if current paradigms are not yielding the results that you crave.

You can overcome any weakness or struggle—and you will. You can bounce back and create the life you want to live if you have been broken or defeated. You are not stuck. If you struggle with addiction and substance abuse, I want you to know that you can become clean and sober. If you struggle with your body image, I want you to know that you can achieve peace. If you struggle in a relationship with desire and communication, I want you to know that you can rekindle the flame, find passion for one another, and communicate at a higher level.

*To achieve it, you just need to see it first,*
*and you can do that through imagination.*

I'm truly not concerned with where you were or even where you are. I'm here to help with where you are going. *Live the Life You Deserve* is a moment in your life where your evolution is about to expand and, perhaps, multiply.

Each instance will require effort, attention, energy, and most importantly *imagination*.

Imagination ignites the spark of creativity, fuels innovation, and opens doors to personal growth and self-transformation. It is through imagination that we harness the power to mold and shape our reality, shaping our aspirations and constructing our highest self. How do we respond or what do we do if we feel as if we have lost our imagination?

## SOCIAL PRESSURES ON OUR IMAGINATION

I feel hypocritical writing this next line as a problem-solving man, an analytical realist, and a professional author whose job is to dissect meaning and definitions in order to craft a mental image for our readers:

*The first step to reconnect with your imagination
is to stop taking everything literally and to
stop judging everything as good or bad.*

The reason we judge everything is for survival. Kids are allowed to play and imagine they are jumping over lava in their bedroom. Yes, my son can be Spider-Man all day and night because I have provisioned a life around him where he is safe, protected, and cared for. Every adult has some major responsibility, such as managing a household or making sure other people survive and thrive. Every parent knows that stress of needing to do something or sacrificing another thing for their kid. All these real-world tasks and concerns can remove us from play, from wonder, from imagination.

We become more "effective" as we get older, and I believe that having kids forces you to become much more "effective" and "productive" as your margin for error decreases. Our brains focus more on things, boundaries, and providing. We become a prisoner to success and work. We often adapt strategies to find "what works," and this gets us further away from frolicking through dandelion fields with face paint on. And, lastly, each society has certain expectations of its elders and adults, and leadership and maturity are expected as one grows up.

Because of social learning, we become conditioned to grow. As we go through major life stages (birth, childhood, adolescence, young adulthood, etc.), our social conditioning causes us drop the bottles, then the imaginary friends, then teenage exuberance. We become more practical. "Responsibility" becomes a bigger part of our identity as we are held to standards around chores, money management, and schoolwork. And then, you suddenly are thrust into adulthood with all its expectations and baggage. This conditioning isn't good or bad—it just is, and the casualty of it all is the magic of our imagination.

*So, what does this mean? Are we supposed*
*to just get serious, pay bills, and die?*

*That's life?*

Look around . . .

Are people who wake up, rush to work, grind all day, and then come home exhausted actually happy? I don't know too many people living this pattern who actually are content. And, sure, I buy that happiness is a fleeting emotion like anything else. However, I have chosen to live the life *I deserve*. To me, that means I deserve to feel happiness every single day. Don't you?

I can't buy into that grind—can you? I need more than that.

## SEEING INTO MY FUTURE

Phoenix, Arizona, 2013. It was a few years after the end of my football career and that open mic night in Chicago. I was a manager at Verizon Wireless with a team of employees I was responsible for, and my career was moving fast due to my results and sales record. I was the leader who made sure we hit metrics and thrived. I held people accountable and made the company a lot of money. I was always available for my career because I "knew" that as long as I had money, I would be "happy."

And I felt *stuck*.

That winter I wanted to return home to Chicago, Illinois, for Thanksgiving and Christmas to be with family. I value family, friendship, and connection more than most other things in life, so my heart dropped when my district manager told me that I would be required to work over the holidays.

I couldn't sit with, accept, and process that another man was making a decision on how I could spend my time. I became angry. My blood bubbled as I thought about what I'd be getting (making time-and-a-half pay) versus what I'd be sacrificing (laughing with my friends and family). I dealt with an inner crisis: this career and money are what I *thought* I needed to be happy, but being with my family is what I *knew* I needed to be happy.

That inner conflict in that moment helped me dive into my imagination to see a different reality. I saw myself in the future working at my current job, feeling guilty about not going to see my family and friends when my soul was screaming at me that I needed to. I saw another version of myself in Chicago full of happiness and joy because I was honest with myself and chose to follow my heart for the holidays. Then I saw another version of myself in a career I was passionate about, still missing my family but accepting the sacrifice as necessary for the benefits my work brought me.

I left that conflict with two new conclusions:

- I can miss certain things that are important to me, but the compensation needs to be worth it.

- I can create any reality I want if I imagine it— if I close my eyes and picture how I will feel.

I put my big-boy pants on and told my manager straight up that I give everything I have to my career. I show up early and stay late. I overwork, overgive, and dedicate myself to my work. Therefore, when I want something, I need to honor what I want—it's that simple to me. And one of my biggest values is friends and family.

Living the life I deserve means honoring what I want. I extend that same invitation for your journey. Get back to living in alignment with your value system.

I am happy to report that I did make it to Chicago that holiday season—and it was the last one I was able to spend with my father. We healed our relationship, and we were able to share laughter, love, and good times. It brings a tear of joy to me today because I am proud of my younger self for sticking to my values and for using my imagination to lean in to a way out of a deep conflict.

Life is fragile, and there is an invitation for you to honor what you hold sacred and for you to use your beautiful mind so it can conjure up situations and outcomes that serve you on the highest levels.

I offer you this story as a reminder of the following.

- Life is fragile; honor your value system and what you consider sacred.
- Imagination during high-conflict times can free you and offer solutions.
- See the end, and allow your imagination of what will be or may be guide you.

## 5 BIG IDEAS TO REMEMBER WHEN CREATING THE LIFE YOU DESERVE

Give yourself permission to think bigger than you are right now. Most people's problem is that they are not thinking big enough, and as a consequence, they take small actions and think very little about themselves. Think bigger.

### 1. You Don't Need "Proof" to Create Something Out of Nothing

You may be looking for proof or data to create a desired outcome or experience in your life, but it may not be present. Activate your imagination and creativity when you are looking to make changes to your life. Athletes at the highest level imagine themselves making the championship-clinching play. Research shows that a positive imagination has a higher chance of creating that perceived outcome.

Transforming your relationships, finances, wellness, and other pillars in life require a willingness to dream. Start now: Imagine yourself arriving at the end goal you desire. Imagine yourself committed to the journey of creating said desire. Imagine what it feels like to be in the process. Then take action today.

When you don't have data and proof, lean in to the thing that we all used as kids: our ability to imagine and see what is not present. Dream big and take actions that are in alignment with that dream, and you'll get there.

## 2. You Will Have to Face Fear and the Unknown

There are no easy answers to life. We find who we are through trial and error. Growth and abundance lie in our ability to remain open to the unknown too. No matter how much research, planning, and organizing you do, there will still be varying degrees of fear and unknown in just about any quest.

*Fear is normal. It is the oldest and strongest emotion that is deeply woven into our subconscious.*

If you're standing at the edge of fear or unknown, or a combination of the two, now is the time to embrace your curiosity. A commitment to learning and openness should be the theme of the month. Make a commitment to take just two steps forward into the unknown each day. You will have to face your fears of what may come as they come.

## 3. Have the Audacity to Dream Big

Take the word *little* out of your speech when you talk about your dreams and aspirations. This is not an exercise in being arrogant but instead an invitation into your greatness and power. So many people have been taught to dream small, to think minor, and to think so little about themselves.

Your ancestors did not go through everything they went through for you to play it small today. We owe it to those who paved a way for us to carry their torch, to create our own, and to make it better for those who may pick up our lead and energy. Have the audacity to think big, take big actions, and dream big as you create the life you deserve.

### 4. Channel Your Energy

One of the ethics of a yoga practice is called *brahmacharya*, a Sanskrit word that means "highest and best use of energy or pure conduct" per Britannica.[1] Brahmacharya is about keeping a certain ethical code to your life by being mindful of all activities and mindsets so you can be intentional with your energy. Indulgence in excess and excessive restraint can both leech your vital energy, resulting in feelings of insecurity and anxiety. The middle path enables you to relish the management of your senses, preventing unbridled desires from tarnishing your enjoyment of life.

Have boundaries with people, places, and things that extract your energy and attention. Commit to pouring into the cups that fill up your life's mission, cups that help you live in alignment with the values that make you prosper.

### 5. Say Yes!

Honor the power that exists within each one of your yeses. To create the life you deserve, you must be open to seizing opportunities that come your way—and you'll have to create your own opportunities. Saying yes means embracing the unknown and stepping into the realm of possibility.

Saying yes isn't about saying yes to *everything* that comes your way but saying yes to the things that align with your purpose, values, and dreams. These opportunities may not always arrive with a clear road map or an abundance of proof, but they often carry the potential to transform your life in profound ways.

When you say yes to the right opportunities, you open the door to growth, change, and fulfillment. It's in those moments when you choose to step into the unknown that you truly expand your horizons. The fear that might accompany such decisions is a sign that you're pushing your boundaries and growing as a person.

Saying yes isn't just about taking risks; it's about recognizing the chances that can propel you toward your aspirations. As you journey through life, keep in mind that some of the most remarkable experiences and transformations come from having the audacity to say yes. Say yes, and say it with a smile. Allow yourself to feel worthy of the life you are creating, and live your life to the fullest.

## IMAGINATION: THE TOOL FOR YOUR NEXT BREAKTHROUGH

Albert Einstein, the iconic figure renowned for his contributions to modern physics and groundbreaking scientific thinking, had an intriguing and somewhat unexpected connection to the world of cycling. There are photographs from his time California, cheerfully pedaling his way through life. He once said, "Life is like riding a bicycle. To keep your balance, you must keep moving." This phrase hints at his connection to riding bicycles and how it sparked his imagination and creativity.

It's believed that one of his most remarkable discoveries, the theory of relativity, was born during one of these rides. As Einstein himself put it, "I thought of it while riding my bicycle." This revelation raises an intriguing question: What is the connection between physical action, imagination, and extraordinary creativity?

The answer lies in the interplay of action and imagination. When we mentally visualize an action, the brain activates the same regions responsible for executing that action. This phenomenon taps into muscle memory and reinforces the neural pathways linked to the desired skill. Visualization also has a profound impact on mindset and emotions. It empowers us to envision success, builds confidence, and shapes the subconscious mind.

When we consistently visualize positive outcomes, our subconscious begins to accept them as attainable possibilities. This shift in mindset influences our thoughts and actions, driving up motivation, enhancing focus, and nurturing the perseverance needed to reach our goals. Albert Einstein's experiences riding his bicycle offer a compelling case study of this connection. The bicycle rides served as a vessel for his imagination, where his creative ideas took root.

I propose that every single day we all activate our imagination with movement by going for a walk, or a run, or cycle. A walk is the most accessible activity, but you could also do yoga, lifting, swimming, or other exercise. I can personally vouch for the benefits of walking based on my own experiences. Stanford researchers found that walking boosts creative inspiration. They examined people while they walked versus while they sat and found that a person's creative output increased by an average of 60 percent when walking. Whether a person was walking outside or on a treadmill inside while staring at a boring blank wall, they still registered double the creative responses as a person sitting. This even surprised the researchers, who thought an interesting setting (being outside) would have more of an effect. The study also found that creative juices continued to flow even when a person lay back down shortly after a walk. This study did not report that focused thinking benefited from walking.[2]

So what do we do with this data? I see the connection between the desire we have when we want to change our life, when we need new ideas and outlets or new pathways or possibilities. I see a commitment to movement and imagination as a direct pathway out.

If you want to 10x your life, use the biggest secret:

*mental and physical movement + a BIG imagination = 10x opportunities*

In fact, I have a story about one of my favorite athletes and humans that illustrates this framework.

## HOW TO BREAK THROUGH BY USING IMAGINATION

My favorite basketball player growing up was Kobe Bryant from the Los Angeles Lakers. He represented work ethic, tenacity, and winning above all else—traits that I admired deeply. I found someone at a young age who represented what was genuine and true to my journey.

In 2008, he had to change in business, mindset, and physical practice in order to create the second act of his basketball career. These nuanced changes launched an incredible trajectory as a business owner, athlete, and father.

By 2008 he had reached the pinnacle of his career. He had won three championships and was considered one of the best basketball players in the world. On December 11, 2009, Kobe's Lakers were 18–3 and they had just beat the

Minnesota Timberwolves 104–92 in a home game. When Kobe went to visit trainer Gary Vitti for clarity on an injury to his right index finger, the X-rays revealed a fracture. He was told that all they could do was tape and splint the finger so he could continue playing. As a right-handed basketball player, that meant Kobe would face torturous pain every time the ball hit his finger: blocking a shot, initiating a steal, catching the ball, and even when he made a pass or shot the ball.

Kobe turned to his imagination to change everything he worked on and built up so he could continue to thrive. In his memoir, *Mamba Mentality*, he detailed the exact process.

> *After I injured my right index finger in the 2009–2010 season, I knew my usual method would no longer work. Up until then, I'd always shot off of my first two fingers. After I hurt it, I had to start focusing on using my middle finger. The middle became my point of release, and I had to sort of let my index finger drift.*
>
> *Making that change took a couple of practices. Not average practices, though. Days flooded with mental and physical work. I had to mentally download the software that was the new form, and then drill it in. I definitely got my one thousand makes in on each of those days.*
>
> *People ask me if the change impacted my shot, if it made me a better or worse shooter. I can't answer that. I can say that there are times when my index finger just went numb, when it had no feeling in it at all. I can also say that was still good enough to win another championship—and that's the only thing that matters.*[3]

Kobe went on to lead the Lakers to three more championship appearances and won two of the three. He also led Team USA to an Olympic gold medal. At the time of his retirement in 2016, he was one of the most successful in his era—and he had to literally change the backbone of his game, his shooting form, in the middle of his career. Changing your form is a big deal and, for some, impossible. Examples like this serve as proof that through imagination, through downloading information in our minds, we can integrate changes to yield the results we deserve.

I love how he noted that he made 1,000 shots per day after he committed to the change. This illustrates two principles that are essential to creating the life we deserve: neuroplasticity, which is our ability to rewire and change our brain's pathways, and the willingness to commit to what you see in your imagination.

## FORMING NEW HABITS: VISUALIZATION IN PRACTICE

At the time of this writing, my son is three years old and embracing the process of learning to get his shoes on, zip and button things properly, and put things back where they belong. As adults we don't really think about the learning process of new habits because we have formed so many. However, as we look to evolve, grow, and live the life we deserve, the core of this work is breaking habits and forming new ones.

Whenever we are learning new habits, we may struggle with the execution of them, and that is normal. My son will attempt to put shoes on, and it won't go as planned. He'll get frustrated and say, "I can't do it." Then he'll give up. As his leader I cannot allow him to get harnessed in the negative language about what he cannot do simply because the language he is using is not factual. I can see that he is so close to getting the shoes on. The only reason he is not getting it right 100 percent of the time is simply because he hasn't practiced enough—the analogy from our Kobe story is that my son has not made his 1,000 shots yet. He must keep shooting. He must keep trying. I want my son to be resilient and to know that he can overcome struggles, so I'll say, "Stop saying what you can't do. Allow yourself to try and fail."

Most importantly I want my son to empower himself for greatness with his inner language, so I give him the positive affirmation of "I can do this. It's not time to give up. It's time to keep trying and to get new information if the information I have is not serving me. I can see myself doing this."

He's heard me say at least a hundred times, "See yourself doing it. You can do it, just keep practicing. It's okay if you don't get it right. Just see yourself doing it. Imagine yourself doing it." I say something along those lines over and over, no matter how many times he fails. This conditions his inner voice to be encouraging—to tap into his imagination and see, feel, and call in the success that will come.

Just the other day, my son told me, "Back up, Daddy. I can put my shoes on by myself." Oh, well, excuse me, son. After a few tries, and without any input from me, he muttered under his breath, "See yourself doing it." Then the shoe slid over the back of his heel. Excitement took over my entire body—it was proof that imagination and visualization work. I knew it worked in my life, but now I was able to see it play out as a leader, coach, and parent.

## BE 10X MORE SPECIFIC

If you hired me to be your coach, I would listen to you talk about your goals, dreams, and what you want to create. You would be vague and bland as you tell me—most people are. The first thing I would then tell you to do is to be 10x more specific. A lot of people have a hard time doing this as they are not used to practicing going bigger and more specific with their thoughts and desires.

This is what happens every single time. People are too vague with their dreams—it often sounds like fear, a lack of belief, and a lack of imagination. Just by following the prompt to be specific, you give yourself 10x better opportunities to manifest, create, and align with the life you want to create.

I am working with a client now, Jeremy, who has three major problems by his own admission.

1.  He feels unwell and is not enjoying being in his body.

2.  He doesn't get enough time with his wife because of work and kids.

3.  He is suffering with deep sadness as a consequence of the first two issues.

After speaking with him, I noticed he repeated the same thing over and over. He was trapped inside the pattern of a few psychological schemas: failure, self-sacrifice, and negativity/pessimism. (Let me be clear, I am not a therapist, so I asked him to consider these after explaining to him what they were. He took the suggestions to his therapist, and she agreed.)

When you have multiple thought processes that are limiting, it can be tricky to work around; however, there is always a solution. On a video call I asked Jeremy, "So how do you see yourself getting out of this situation?"

His response was frank and blunt. "I can't see the blueprint for how I am going to do this."

I said, "When you use the word *blueprint,* it is making me think that you are looking for an instruction booklet, like when we buy a new television or electronic device. I need you to understand that this won't be a play-by-play but instead a new commitment to two things: a new mindset and a new lifestyle. You will only get out of this hole with these two things: First, a declaration of exactly what you want and how you will make your first move. Second, a commitment to your highest self. You have permission to choose what your declaration is, but you need a phrase, a goal, a statement, or some spoken desire that is going to guide you."

He cut me off and said, "What is your highest self?"

I explained what I thought the highest self was for me, and I told him that it's imperative we each define highest self for ourselves. The exercise that we did in the last chapter is what I did with him right there. I would argue that answering what it means to be in your highest self is the path to enabling your imagination.

I continued, "To do this exercise, you need to be in your creative brain. Instead of looking for a map to where you want to go, *start at the end.* Imagine your highest self one year from now. What did he do differently? How did he arrive at this point? What are some of the things he stopped doing to arrive at this point? I want you to imagine that version of yourself. I want you to feel it. I want you to close your eyes and see what is already inside of you manifest, grow, and blossom right out of your brain and heart."

He took a deep breath to drop into this request.

*He thought; he felt.*

*He could see it.*

*He could feel it.*

This is one of the hardest parts of living the life you deserve, when you have to call yourself out for what you've been doing and how you've been living. When you need to recognize your poor decisions, your self-sabotage, and the destructive behavior that limits you from survival, from thriving, or living in alignment the way you crave. This is one of the most important parts of the journey.

This is the work—it can't be skipped.

After a moment of deep thought, Jeremy looked back at me and said, "I have to be better with my snacking habit. It's just that simple; I have to be better. When I get down on myself, I turn to fake food and sugary snacks, and I overdo it every single time."

"What else? Tell me more."

"I have to make time for me. I have to make time to move more. I have to make time and prioritize my health."

"Be more specific—that's vague," I said.

"I have to go for more walks. I need to get back to playing hockey once a week with my mates. I need to lift some weights a few times a week. I need to move my body more when I'm working."

I said, "Those things you just named, are they sustainable, are they things you actually enjoy?"

"Yes," he said.

"Okay, I like that. Now add one more thing to that equation that you don't enjoy. What is something that causes discomfort, that is hard, that you can add? I love you doing a bunch of things you want, but we need a challenge. We need to also integrate hard things into this new lifestyle, at least one hard thing that you can commit to. It doesn't have to be recurring, but it does need to be hard."

He looked at me like he wanted to slap me. I kept a straight face and let him think. A minute later, he said, "I should sign up for a marathon. I used to run half marathons a while ago, and they kept me in shape. I've been wanting to do a marathon but just lost so much confidence in myself. It will be hard, and I don't want to do it . . . but I *do* want to do it. Does that make any sense?"

I laughed and said, "Oh yes, I love this for you. Something hard, something beyond what you are capable of in this moment. I don't know anything about running marathons, so please tell me you know how to set up a plan for that. I can then hold you accountable to the plan you come up with. Get me the plan by our next meeting, and I can hold you to the progress until it's time. Hell, I'll even fly to you when you run to support you on race day."

"Deal. Sylvester, you have a deal." Jeremy grinned.

I said, "I like this plan and I like this direction, but there's one small thing I want you to do. I want you to be mindful of your inner voice and your mindset.

"Self-sacrifice is the belief that you should voluntarily, and often excessively, give up your own needs for the sake of others. Sometimes, you can self-sacrifice who you are, your goals, and your dreams for your family. But is that the message you want to send? Taking care of your health is the pathway for us to teach our kids self-love and for us to show our partners that we want them to be inside of their greatness too.

"Neglecting yourself is the result of this mindset. If this belief does not change, your life will not change. So, I want to offer you this new belief: I will make sacrifices for my family to give them the life they deserve, *and* I will make sacrifices for my health and wellness to give me the life I deserve.

"Can you accept this as your new focal point? Can you use this language that allows you more space and compassion as a parent, while allowing you to still be a giver and servant to your family? Do you recognize that you matter too and that your personal wellness goals matter?"

Tears started to flow at this point. He left the call with a great deal of energy, a plan, and a new mental model to focus on. I told him that he should focus on the childhood wounds that caused his schemas in his next talk with his therapist, but his new game plan for dealing with them could work as a band-aid until the wounds adequately healed.

# JOURNAL PROMPTS:
# SPARK IMAGINATION

- When it comes to goals, dreams, plans, and all
  the things we want most, people are often vague.
  Specifically write down what you want, how it will
  happen, what you will do, and what you will sacrifice.
  Leave no detail unexamined. This exercise isn't meant
  for you to overthink or to put "too much" on your
  shoulders. This is so you can get momentum, energy,
  and specific details behind what you crave most. Yes,
  life will play out as it will, and you will have to adjust
  and adapt. No, the plan does not have to be rigid. But
  you do need something today.

- Start at the end. Most people get "stuck" when they
  are dreaming or coming up with what they want
  because they think about the now and the idea of
  starting just feels overwhelming. Reverse-engineer
  the process and start at the end. Start with the end
  emotions. Start with the end situation. Start with the
  end goal. And then, once you have a clear mental
  image of the end, start from there.

- What is the new habit that you must start that aligns
  with this journey? There could be 100 new habits.
  For today just pick one to commit to. Is it going to
  bed earlier? Is it studying at the library for two hours
  every Friday? Is it a daily writing goal of 45 minutes?
  Is it going to the gym every day? Pick one new habit.
  The purpose of picking one new habit is that it helps
  you with neuroplasticity—the ability to rewire your
  brain. Be specific. What is the one habit that you must
  start today?

Fall in love with the depth of your imagination. The most dangerous thing we can do is stop dreaming, stop believing, and lose hope in possibility or change. Get back to being a kid again around how you view your life. Romanticize and play with your life like the game that it is. Society is training us all to be serious, to be so determined and focused that every day passes us by. Stop. Enjoy this life and integrate fun at every opportunity. We are here to play, frolic, and fall in love with the depths of who we can become.

— **Sylvester McNutt III,** *Live the Life You Deserve*

I need more people to understand this: you can create images and ideas in your mind that then become true in real life. Thoughts can become things. When I was 18 years old at college, I knew I wanted to write books that could change people's lives. That was a thought, and this book is a thing—the law of attraction is real. Using your imagination to design your life is a real tool. Write your goals and dreams down daily. Put them somewhere where you can see them, and track the actions associated with them.

— **Sylvester McNutt III,** *Live the Life You Deserve*

When we are thinking about our dreams and our goals, overthinking can occur— and damn, does that feel like a weight to carry. Overthinking often has to do with holding on to too many thoughts, which means some of what you are processing *doesn't matter*. Identify what is truly important and let go of the rest.

— **Sylvester McNutt III,** *Live the Life You Deserve*


Thinking more has never helped me solve an overthinking issue. Going for a walk and journaling has always helped. Getting clear on what I value and what I want always helps. If you are overthinking, stop. Leave your phone at home and go for a walk.

— **Sylvester McNutt III,** *Live the Life You Deserve*

CHAPTER 3

# THE MAGIC OF
# CONFRONTING THE PREDATOR

To design the life you want, you'll have to engage in conflict, and you'll have to learn how to manage conflict.
At some point, you will have to destroy the predator that is
in your life. Until you slay the predator, it may have a psychological control over you. There are a million and one
ways to engage in conflict. Creating the life you deserve will
create conflict, and you cannot hide from it.

Healing comes after the confrontation. The initiation of healing gives us access to more power, more space, more energy for creating the life we deserve to live.

— **Sylvester McNutt III,** *Live the Life You Deserve*

We will hurt people we love, we will be rude and unfair, and we will make what we will later refer to as mistakes. All relationships will experience varying degrees of conflict and infraction. There will come repair and recovery after the rain of those seasons. We can only create the life we deserve by integrating our shadow, our darkness, the pages about our story that we like to pretend are not there.

— **Sylvester McNutt III,** *Live the Life You Deserve*

As we meander through this journey of living the life we deserve, it would serve us for this chapter to keep with the theme of imagination. Please accept and acknowledge that the concept of predator here is using mystical language; it is not literal. The Western mind wants to use its imagination, but our collective consciousness now is largely literal. Let's stay in the imaginative world of the mythical with the sole purpose of adding more language to our journey. Language that is fuller and capable of describing what we may be entering or leaving. This language can be used to make our situation lighter, to help us look at it in a different way, to even add more layers to how we are defining our experience.

When humans used to live outside, there were real, physical predators that we had to slay, fight, and learn to survive with. At this point in modern society, for the most part, we are not facing real danger to that degree every day. For most people, their lives are safe. That is a blessing for which we can send gratitude and thanks to our ancestors for their hard work and sacrifices. It's not hyperbole to assume that someone gave their life for us to have what we have today.

Some of the dangers that we face and that feel real to us are our predators, and they can show up in many different forms. Luckily, someone has overcome the very things each one of us are struggling with. And, even better, there is so much support, love, and guidance available to us as we confront and engage the predator. As a self-mastery coach, author, father, and athlete, I have seen thousands of people not live up to their potential because of the fear of said predator. I don't want that for you or me, so where do we begin? I believe the starting point is acceptance: we must encounter our predator. In that confrontation, we will find healing, courage, strength, confidence, transformation, and a path out!

We cannot allow the predator to stop us from living the life we deserve. For some people the predator is a bad spending habit; for others it's the ex who has emotional control over them; and for some people it's a mindset pattern that needs to be reframed and redirected. A predator can take many forms and energies, so let's define it for the sake of clarity. Once we name it, we can claim it. And once we recognize and, in some cases, claim ownership, that sort of accountability gives us access to the empowering choices to release, let go, or build healthy boundaries with said predator.

## WHAT IS THE PREDATOR?

*"One does not become conscious by imagining figures of light, but by making the darkness conscious."*

— Carl Jung, *Alchemical Studies*

Carl Jung stressed that our goal is not perfection but wholeness through integration of the shadow. He once said, "By not being aware of having a shadow, you declare a part of your personality to be nonexistent. Then it enters the kingdom of the nonexistent, which swells up and takes on enormous proportions. . . . If you get rid of qualities you don't like by denying them, you become more and more unaware of what you are, you declare yourself more and more nonexistent, and your devils will grow fatter and fatter."[1] Truthfully, can you afford to allow your devils to grow fatter and fatter? No. For everyone reading this book at the same time, the answer is no; we cannot afford to ignore our shadow, or pain, or predator.

Moving forward, we must release an ideal of perfection, for it does not serve us. As humans, we are not after perfection. In fact, perfection cannot be actualized in the human experience. We will hurt people we love, we will be rude and unfair, and we will make what we will later refer to as mistakes. All relationships will experience varying degrees of conflict and infraction. There will come repair and recovery after the rain of those seasons. We can only create the life we deserve by integrating our shadow, our darkness, the pages of our story that we like to pretend are not there. Your little corporate voice can't save you. You hide and lie at the family gatherings, and those lies can't save you. You fake it on social media to get love, approval, and validation, but you know, and I know, social media cannot save you. Integrating your darkness, your pain, your predator, your fears is the way. And through integration we heal, we reach potential, we release the masks, and we become totally free. You can save yourself through integration of your darker side.

In our mission to live the life we deserve, we are going to encounter roadblocks that will come in a predatory form—that is the truth, and there is no reason to sugarcoat this. Like I said, I use the term *predator* in this book in a poetic, not literal, form. So to explain it, I need to discuss the hero's arc, which essentially states that a protagonist of a story must face his or her inner demons or conflicts. Once they gain mastery of said inner conflict, they will have the skills, strength, or tools necessary to conquer the external conflict, the danger lurking in the shadows of existence.

The predator is an entity, an energy, an idea, and possibly a real person who represents doom and danger, fear and anxiety. Remember yourself as a young kid, your imagination taking you into the corners of your bedroom or behind the closed doors in your closet. You may see a monster, a ghost, or some other figure that preys on your fear and anxiety. You may hide under the covers, hoping it goes away, or sprint down the hallway to grab a parent who represents safety and protection. You may stay there, stuck, paralyzed at the fear of what may be. Depending on your life, conditioning, instincts, and fight-or-flight response, the possible outcomes are endless.

The presence of the predator brings us into a darker place. It keeps us out of alignment with the life we want to live and at a lower vibration of existence. It lives in the shadows of our consciousness as well. The predator is the conversation we won't have aloud. The predator is often that thing or conversation that we avoid but can feel the thick of it even if we remain silent.

## TYPES OF PREDATORS

Francis Weller is a psychotherapist from California, and he has an audio program that I listened to during the 2020 pandemic. It was one of those pieces of media that I didn't even know I needed. In his audio program, "The Alchemy of Initiation," he talks about how something can arise out of the initiations we have in life and how in our path of accepting initiations—which simply means the beginning of something—we will at times have a rough initiation. He says, "The soul keeps bringing us to threshold experiences so we can step into a larger and more encompassing sense of self. A larger identity, capable of tuning in and attending to what soul is asking of us."[2]

I think of this line every single time I must face a predator. The predator exists to invite us into a deeper capacity where we can tune in and attend to life. This initiation expands our narrative. The embrace of this initiation offers expansion of our personal history and makes us feel less isolated.

Francis helped me understand and expand my imagination when he named the predator, "We must take it on because it's often the deepest core that shows us if we have reverence for life. This is not personal. This does not arrive out of your personal wounds. In our Western psychology, we personalize everything. Not everything in the psyche is you. This is about accepting the multiplicity of our experience. The stories tell us that this confrontation is both inevitable and necessary."[3]

Find solace in not taking this personally. Don't assume that you are defective or that something is wrong with you. Your predator might be a toxic person, but there are situations in life, lots of them and most of them, where the predator is not. Yeah, you know that math test that you can never pass? That's a predator. That conversation that you won't have with your husband about that one thing killing your relationship? Yes, that is a predator. When you lie to your friends and family about the cookies and sweets that you sneak and overeat, yes, that is a predator too. If you are a people pleaser, that first conversation about setting boundaries that you avoid is a predator to your progress. You know that nasty spending habit you have? Yes, that is the predator too.

No matter who you are and where you are in life, a great fight will present itself. The young kid who grows up without a mother or father must learn how to heal the absence of that wound. For the person struggling with a sickness, they and their family must learn how to adjust to the condition. If you struggled with, or grew up around, substance abuse, there is a great fight to get sober or have boundaries. There is a person who cannot break the habit of snacking on unhealthy sweets, but they know deep in their heart if they can break this habit, they could unlock the deepest well of health. There is a woman somewhere who simply can't get ahead financially because she feels like she is trapped, yet the truth is she makes more than enough but has a spending problem. Once she comes into connection with this inner predator, then and only then will she be able to change the external experience. There's a guy somewhere who wants to thrive, but he gives too much attention to his gambling addiction. For him to thrive, he needs to confront this predator and get support.

No human being is perfect. We all have something in our story, and as we evolve and grow, we will have to come into connection and engage with future predators. These confrontations are a requirement to thrive, a requirement for growth. I want to empower you with the tools to do so.

## A PRACTICAL EXAMPLE FOR WORKING WITH THE PREDATOR

I have no problem being vulnerable and sharing these stories because I have conquered the predators that have come to destroy me, and I know that through testimony we can all grow and transform.

I grew up with a physically abusive parent, and part of my survival strategy was to maneuver in a way that would result in my body not being physically attacked by my father. I had to find ways to adapt until I was strong enough to defend myself. To keep myself out of the house and out of his way, I played sports, started working at McDonald's when I was 14 years old, and spent as much time as possible at my friends' and cousin's houses.

As I got older, however, I knew a confrontation had to come, but I was afraid of engaging the predator. He not only controlled me mentally but also was physically dominant. Once of my first memories is watching my father knock out a man who was trying to break in to our car. He gave him a two-piece combo to the face, and the man fell to the ground behind my father's force. Another time, my father wrestled a gun away from a bigger man and put him into a chokehold. I was in real danger with my father, but he protected us every single time, at all costs. That's what was particularly confusing about my predator. Why does he protect me from everyone else while inflicting pain on me? It was a riddle that I never found the answer for.

I know this may seem like my father was the worst human being of all time, but he was far from it. He was a great man with an unruly mindset toward teaching and discipline. He did not live in fantasy land at all. He was practical, logical, and hard, a truly old-school father who simply wouldn't be on board with half the things this society is okay with. Even though he had his flaws and his own predators, you wouldn't know me or my work without him. So in a way, I am grateful for the entire journey.

I also don't think he interpreted his violence as something traumatic. He came from a different era than what we live in now. He grew up in the racially divided post-war America of the 1960s and 1970s. It was vastly different than my own generation growing up in the 1990s and early 2000s. His generation was hard because they had to be, and they worked hard because they had to. I believe the violence he displayed, in his head, was out of love. He felt it was necessary, and it made up a part of the culture at that time: war, violence, and domination. He wanted me to have the survival skills that he would've needed, that his childhood wounds and schemas told him that I needed.

My father had the abuse schema, which is the belief that others are inclined to be abusive, manipulative, selfish, or intent on causing harm or exploiting you. Trust becomes a challenging prospect with this schema, and he wanted me to develop discernment because of his experience. He wanted me to be wise, to be sharp, to have confidence, and to be so strong that no man or woman would break me. He wanted to cause me pain so I would never be destroyed by the world, wouldn't live in fear, and would be stronger than any enemy. His method worked to a degree. My father had a special way of teaching lessons that always made me feel like I was downloading wisdom from a master—but I did have to undergo a decade of healing to find peace from the journey.

Before my healing journey started, however, I had to confront my father. This was one of the hardest things I had ever done in my life. When I reached 19 years of age, I was torn between anger, sadness, depression, and a deep hatred toward him and the world. I felt like he didn't give me as much love as I needed, while he felt like his job wasn't to love but to guide. I confronted him because he was predatory. The confrontation happened over the phone first as I told him I needed to get things off my chest, and I needed him to address my concerns. Then later, we met over a meal, and I cleared the air even more. This was my initiation to my healing journey. I was able to confront the person I felt gave me the most pain.

My father's response does not matter because he did not need to validate me, and I hope you understand that for your journey. It would be great if your predator could validate you, but that is not the goal. The goal is to simply engage the confrontation. To be clear, I named that he abused me physically. Confrontation for me did not mean getting even, fighting, or hurting him. Confrontation for me was using my powerful words to look him in the eyes and to make him aware of the pain he caused. My great work was developing the courage to have a conversation, an honest and direct one, with the man I feared. I did it, and that is when my freedom began.

*Healing comes after the confrontation.*

*The initiation of healing gives us access to more power, more space, more energy for creating the life we deserve to live.*

Remember, at this point in the story, one person's predator was a conversation with someone. This is simply an example. A predator in your life may look different.

## THE CONSEQUENCES OF NOT ENGAGING THE PREDATOR

If you are used to avoiding conflict, then you have allowed certain problems to exist longer than necessary. These are some of the consequences you might face by not engaging with your predator:

- Living in fear, hiding, playing small
- Creating more fear when it's unneeded
- A landscape of little to no confidence
- Running from grit, mental fortitude, and self-confidence
- Small thinking, unable to imagine something different or better

- Running from freedom and choosing a more enslaved path
- Nervous system is consistently triggered
- Stress and anxiety at an all-time high, maybe even depression

If you choose to avoid your own predators, it's possible that you might retreat and hide and create safety that way. But ignoring your spending problem doesn't make the debt go away. Avoiding your food addiction doesn't increase your health and vitality. There is so much power on the other side of attacking your problems.

Let go of the avoidant energy inside you. Understand and accept that you have what it takes to find solutions, to be creative and find a way out. See yourself as someone who has the power and ability to resolve conflicts and issues. If you are a spiritual person, then understand that you have the power of surrender as well, and surrender is not a passive approach. You can surrender to God or to the universe. You can surrender and ask for help and guidance. You can surrender to a mentor or to a coach who can lead you out of this conflict. Fall in love with the process of surrendering when the time comes. Know that you have enough energy to move through the problems that arise.

As a consequence of not engaging my father when I was younger, I felt weaker and trapped. I can look back now and know that it wasn't true safety, but it was all I could do at the time. I felt like he would literally kill me if he wanted to. I knew in my heart that I had to create an engagement with him. But first, I had to prepare to fight the predator.

## HOW TO PREPARE FOR AN ENGAGEMENT WITH THE PREDATOR

**Disclaimer:** If you are in a seriously dangerous situation, the most appropriate course of action may be to contact support, help, family, or the authorities. Even though I shared a real-life experience of engaging with my physical predator, I don't want you to think that I am telling you that you must fight with a person who is unsafe.

This topic of the predator is one that I am approaching from myth, from imagination, from a creative standpoint. It is an allegory, an analogy for real-life experiences. It can be deep if you want it to have that meaning, and it can be shallow if that fits. For example, I'm sharing a deeper meaning related to a childhood wound, but I could easily share a lighter meaning and tell you that the Chicago Bears football franchise ruins my happiness every Sunday. They are my predators since I cheer for them, and all they do is lose and lose more. See, this language can be playful, deep, or shallow, and that is why I love it because it gives us more agency for telling our narrative.

If you are faced with a physical predator, these mindset exercises may be done on your own, without involving them, in order to prepare yourself mentally for removing yourself from the dangerous situation with professional support, if needed.

### Step 1: You Have to Make Your Declaration

When we are dealing with inner battles, we must make a declaration of yes and a declaration of no. So much of our life is about patterns, and when we are looking to make massive changes, we must look at the language that we are using. Saying yes or saying no are powerful words. The things we say yes and no to have the power to keep us alive, to allow us to thrive, to bring in joy and love. And of course, the inverse is true as well.

When I was a personal trainer, I had a guy come to me who was 350 pounds. During our onboarding process, I asked why he wanted to hire me, and he said, "I can't be this big anymore. I am saying no more to hiding sodas and lying about what I am eating. I need help to thrive. No more."

That declaration right there set a demarcation in his brain; it breaks the pattern. He said no to his unhealthy state, no to his bad habits, and yes to thriving.

When you are looking to confront the predator, there is both a yes and no that must occur. For most of us, the no is where the freedom is going to exist.

### Step 2: Embrace Conflict from an Integrated and Safe Energy Field

We must recognize that conflict is not something that is always bad and needs to be avoided. However, nothing productive will come of the confrontation unless you go within and do the work necessary to approach your predator from a healed place. When we do the work of integrating our shadows, our energy field becomes a safe place.

Recently, one of my coaching clients, Travis, was attempting to date his ex-girlfriend after not seeing her for two years. They had decided to part ways because of personal differences and their lack of healthy communication amid the shores of conflict. As their conflict was boiling, she spent time and space with another guy, which hurt him and led to their breakup.

After the breakup, he did a lot of inner work, saw a therapist, trained in Thailand to sharpen his brain and body, and focused solely on growing and healing. I was apprehensive about him getting back with her because I'd listened to his journey every two weeks over that two-year period. But I felt confident in his tools and mindset, and I knew that if we moved from the right energy space and mindset, then anything was possible.

One night Travis called me from a trip he was taking with her and said, "Sylvester, the first three days were perfect, but today there's been some issues. We are supposed to spend five days together, but I'm thinking about leaving now."

He explained that she was putting pressure on him to "be with her," and he was uncomfortable with that. He wanted her to learn this newer healed version of him first, without pressure.

I said, "You obviously want to be with her, but you're wanting her to learn this new you, to get to know this version of you rather than the person she knew from two years ago—and you need to honor that. This is a confrontation with fire. She is calling you into the threshold, she is calling you forward, and it's causing an inner conflict. You don't know if she is safe for you because she left you for someone else.

"At this moment, it's important that you activate your throat chakra and honor your voice. You called me to share because I am the safe space, but in your heart, you want her to be a safe space too. The only way that will happen is if you embrace the conflict, if you embrace and engage the fire of this moment. As a leader, you have to be tactful, you can't scream or yell, but you need to be direct and tell her exactly what you want and why you want it.

She hurt you, and you're allowed to make sure she is a safe space before you 'be with her' as she is asking for. Are you ready to have this conversation?"

He said, "Thank you, Sylvester. This is what I needed to hear. And yes, I will have a conversation with her tonight."

On our next meeting, Travis came in and said, "Thank you for the game and direction you gave me. I declared that we would not continue how we used to and that there was a new way for us to communicate. I respected my commitment to my highest self, and she respected me as well. The trip ended well, and we will be seeing each other again soon."

This healing was possible because they confronted the predator together, but he had to go within first and acknowledge the fire that was inside of him.

### Step 3: Recognize that Change Has to Happen with Habits or Mindset

Sometimes, a predator is our own mindset or habits that are keeping us stuck. To prepare for this type of confrontation, we must be willing to look within and take accountability for the part we are playing.

For instance, I have a client who is a retired school-teacher. Janice has a great relationship with her husband, her kids are grown and in healthy relationships, she has great health, and she is a millionaire. In our society, we'd consider her a "success," yet she feels stuck. She feels dis-engaged; she feels lost at sea. And here's the thing, there is nothing wrong with being lost at sea. It's okay to wander, to wonder, to be curious about life and explore the angles of existence. In her story, her predator is her mindset.

In this Western society, we are conditioned to identify who we are as what we do within our careers. It's one of the first questions asked when you meet someone—and it's a question that I hate: "Oh, what do you do?" It simply means, "What is your job?" Is this truly the most pressing thing you want to know about people? To me, that's a joke of a question.

My indifference here exists because I do not define my human worth based on my career. This is not a slight to my hard work and dedication; I love what I have built and honor the people who have empowered my success. I'm signed to the top personal development publishing company in the world, Hay House, and I'm one of the most sought-after self-mastery coaches in the world. But on a soul level, there's so much more to me.

When I shared this perspective with my client, it allowed her to unlock a new perspective for herself. She was able to deconstruct the mindset that was causing her to feel stuck. Her confrontation was simply about getting a fresh perspective and taking pieces of it that served her.

That's the power of the predator: it makes you feel like you are not enough, like what you are doing is somehow not the right path, and like there's a war happening inside your psyche. In this situation, I don't consider this predator bad. I try not to look at it as solely good or bad. If you remove the good and bad judgments, everything in life gets so much easier to manage. In her case, the predator is here to open her wide, to allow her to grow into a new version of herself—and in this situation, the predator is safe and glorious.

In the next chapter, we will continue the work of facing the predator, embracing conflict, and preparing ourselves to mythically fight with what may have us feeling stuck or uneasy.

# JOURNAL PROMPTS:
# EMBRACING THE PREDATOR

- Do you have a predator in your life? If so, what is it?

- It is often said that the next level will require us to get through something. What is it that you need to get through?

- If you create a declaration about attacking this predator, what does that language sound like? Is there anyone who will witness and support you? For example, "The predator in my life is sugar, and I want and need my partner to support me and help me in this journey of going sugar-free."

- What would happen if you broke up with being avoidant and embraced conflict? Is it possible that you would end the conflict and move on faster?

- Write freely on the concept of understanding that this is not personal. It is not an attack on you. The recognition of a problem in your life does not mean you are not worthy of greatness; it means you are called to resolve conflict. Write freely about not taking things personally and how it feels when you do versus when you don't.

You will have the same lessons and problems presented to you over and over until you engage your shadow, until you have self-awareness and take inventory on what is happening and why. Once you bring the unconscious to the conscious, then you can make massive changes.

— **Sylvester McNutt III,** *Live the Life You Deserve*

I need more people to understand this: Running from your problems makes the problems bigger. The quicker you can attack what is attacking you, the quicker you can erase it and get back to living your life. Be dominant when it comes to "your problems." Be ruthless. Be a savage. Be a bully when it comes to "your problems." That is how you get over, through, and around these issues, and this type of energy often mitigates the potential of them returning.

— **Sylvester McNutt III,** *Live the Life You Deserve*

M ost people suffer because they keep their problems to themselves. Your problems are a predator, and they prey on you in isolation. Healing occurs when you embrace the predator, when you let trust and loved ones in, and when you get loving support for your journey.

— **Sylvester McNutt III**, *Live the Life You Deserve*

G ive yourself permission to stop running from your problems. Give yourself permission to ask for help so you can get the love, support, and direction you need. Speaking up and asking for help does not make you weak or dumb; it makes you human. Break up with the pieces of your identity that guilt you into this struggle. There is power in community, collaboration, and teamwork. Creating the life you deserve does not mean you need to do everything on your own. Other people are here to support your dream and best life too. Give them an opportunity to show up for you.

— **Sylvester McNutt III**, *Live the Life You Deserve*

CHAPTER 4

# PREPARING FOR THE GREAT FIGHT

When I tell you to go live the life you deserve, I am also telling you to go fight for your life. I am telling you to fight for what you want, to show up and give it your all. There will be thousands of opportunities in life where you need to fight for what you want, to overcome a struggle, or to confront a mindset or habit that is keeping you from the life you deserve. Prepare yourself for the great fight.

You have overcome everything that was meant to destroy you.

— **Sylvester McNutt III,** *Live the Life You Deserve*

Go to the fight. Engage with your problems, your shadows, and everything that you are afraid of. True transformation is on the other side of the fight.

— **Sylvester McNutt III,** *Live the Life You Deserve*

In sports, you learn that preparing for the fight is more important than the fight itself. When I look at the modern civilized world, I see people who are not willing to engage and fight for the things that they want; they don't prepare for what they want to experience and how they want to feel. If you take anything away from this book, I would love for it to be your commitment to the preparation for the fights of your life. The better you prepare, the better your results will be and the more equipped you will be to handle what is happening to you and around you.

Depending on where you live, the word *fight* may conjure up a variety of emotions. I am challenging you to release any negative connotations that the word *fight* has for the moment because I am not using it in a negative way. I am not literally referring to violence and harm. Again, this is a practice in imagination, a practice in using our beautiful minds to take back control and power with the language that is available to us.

When I use the word *fight*, I am referring to stepping up to the plate and stepping inside your power. I am referring to being accountable and responsible. I am speaking on engaging the conflicts, problems, and bumpy roads in our life. There are a lot of different ways to prepare for a fight, but I feel like each one of us can keep these two principles with us as we prepare to engage:

*Protect Yourself at All Times*

*True Power Is Restraint*

## PROTECT YOURSELF AT ALL TIMES

I grew up in Mount Prospect, Illinois, in a time when kids were outside all day playing sports, doing adventures, and longing for exploration. We played every sport under the sun: futbol, football, tennis, basketball, street hockey, frisbee, and baseball, and we even had swimming competitions.

One game we'd often play was called *Killerman*. It's a simple concept. One person is the "man," and the other 10 players are the "killers." The killers are trying to win by tackling the man. At the start of the game, the man and the killers stand about 40 yards apart. One person on the killers' team throws or kicks the ball as far as he can to whoever is designated as the man. While the ball is being launched, the other killers are running down the field to tackle the man. The man is trying to catch the ball, and his sole objective is to avoid getting tackled and score by crossing the endzone line, which is usually 40 yards or so away. The person with the ball can use stiff-arms and spin moves; he can jump over and even run through people. Of course, we were mimicking what we saw on television when we watched football, but we had no pads, no medics, no trainers—it was just boys being boys. Just a lot of heart, fearlessness, and pure savagery.

One spring day, when I was a young boy, I was out at the park playing *Killerman*. The boys I played with were roughly two years older than me, but I was faster than them, had better vision, and was more agile. As the man, I remember the ball floating to me in the air while the killers ran toward me. After I received the ball, my instincts took over as I juked, shook, and maneuvered around the killers like a squirrel running up a tree. When I reached the endzone seconds later, they were pissed. Reaching

the endzone in *Killerman* hardly happens—maybe 10 percent of the time or less for most people. I was able to get in
there with ease, so they made me go again. The fire in their
eyes was real. *How dare a younger boy outperform the older
ones?* I had no problem going again. I knew I was an elite
athlete as a kid.

As the ball was hurled toward me for my second attempt,
I could feel the energy of redemption in the air. After about
10 seconds or so, the result was the same. I scored. The other
boys were pissed, but one, James, was enraged that I embarrassed him. He didn't say much as he walked up to me, put
both hands on my shoulders, placed his right leg behind my
knees, and pushed me backward. Because of his leg place-
ment, I instantly slammed to the ground.

This was the first time that I got into a "fight," and
initially I didn't really understand what was going on.
My instincts took over, and I heard an inner voice saying,
"Move. Right hand, move. Left hand, move. Move." This
voice inside of me was protecting me. I felt invincible, like
the Greek soldier Achilles at war. A few moments later, the
inner voice turned into my father's deep voice: "Get the f---
off him." I turned slightly as I felt James retreating, and sure
enough there was my dad, picking me up off the ground.

When we got home, I realized my dad had been record-
ing the entire epic event as it played out. He had his camera
on a tripod aimed at the field. The music of his favorite musi-
cian, Michael Jackson, was playing, and lavender candles
were burning, creating an oddly calming vibe throughout
the apartment. He sat me on the brown couch, in between
the lion and tiger sculptures on each endcap, and said, "So
why did that boy want to fight you?"

"I don't know. He couldn't tackle me and didn't like it. I didn't say anything to him," I said as I looked at the floor. I could see the grass and sweat all over my knees.

"Look me in the eyes when you speak. So let me get this straight. He fought you because he couldn't tackle you." My father's eyebrows went up after his inquisition.

"Yes, that's correct, sir." I didn't break eye contact this time. I kept a blank face like a mime. I stayed calm like a napping baby.

He picked up his beer with a small smirk. It's strange. I don't know what he was thinking at that moment, but I felt that he was proud of me.

He took another sip of beer, then said, "The fact that you knew how to move like that without ever playing tells me that you are a natural football player. Would you like to play when we move next year?" This was one of the first memories I have of my father acknowledging me.

I nodded my head in agreement. I watched football with my father just about every Sunday. I learned to copy the movements I observed, and that is what I used on the field.

He followed up. "Now, you need to learn how to fight. I don't ever want to see you get your ass whooped again. Do you hear me?" He said it in a laughing manner, but he was serious.

I nodded my head. "Yes, sir."

"Put your hands up. Look your opponent in the eye. Look at this center point of my chest. You can see every movement they make if you look at this center point. Look me in the eye again. Become completely aware of what is happening. Hear my voice but *feel* the energy beyond it. Feel when I might swing. Feel when I might attack. Do not break eye contact. Look me in the eye.

"The first rule of any fight is to always protect yourself. Do not let your guard down until you are safe. You will know when you are safe. You will block ten punches by moving your hand."

He threw 10 punches at me back-to-back. I couldn't block them all. "Again," he said.

He tossed 10 more punches in the air toward me. "Again."

We did this same drill over and over, and it felt like 75 hours drifted by as I did one drill. In between sets, my father would take a sip of his beer. The music was blasting, but for some reason, it felt silent. When you grow up with loud voices, loud music, and a lot of input, you learn how to tune it out with ease. He wasn't trying to hit me. He was trying to show me that approaching a fight is just about rhythm, confidence, and competence.

Before I was born, my father had his own karate and boxing studio in South Holland, Illinois, for all the kids in the neighborhood. He started it when he got out of the U.S. Army as his way of keeping in shape, staying disciplined, and building relationships with other people in the neighborhood. He trained over 100 teenagers in how to defend themselves physically, mentally, and intellectually.

During the era that they grew up in, racist laws and attitudes were woven through the fabric of United States. To protect themselves, Black Americans at that time leaned heavily into community, into serving one another through various ways like cutting the elders' grass, community lunches, and looking after one another to make sure they were reaching for greatness. My father chose combat sports and intellectual practices like reading, writing, and meditation.

"Protect yourself at all times. When you engage in a fight, you must protect yourself. Do not release your guard until you are safe. Believe that you will be safe. Say it back to me."

I repeated, "Protect yourself at all times. When you engage in a fight, you must protect yourself. Do not release your guard until you are safe. Believe that you will be safe. Say it back to me."

He bellowed with laughter. "Okay, but don't say the 'say it back to me' part."

I smirked back at him. "I'm just trying to follow directions."

It was a moment of lightness in a serious moment. The last thing he said to me that afternoon was, "You might not be able to win every fight, but if you care about your defense, if you protect yourself, that voice in your head and your heart will guide you to safety. Always trust that voice in your head when you need to engage in a fight. Do not hesitate. Do not overthink. You know what safety feels like. When you engage in a fight, protect yourself at all times and trust that you will return to safety."

For the next two months, I trained with my father. He taught me how to get in an athletic stance, how to throw a jab, a hook, and an uppercut. He taught me how to feint, which is to fake a jab before you throw another more devastating punch. He taught me how to mimic the most famous boxer at that time, Mike Tyson, by being light on my feet and moving my head up and down. Now, let me be clear, I am not saying I achieved Mike Tyson's level of skill when it came to boxing; he was merely the inspiration.

Imagination was key in my training. My dad would shadow box with me, which is throwing a bunch of punches in a sequence while you are literally imagining yourself in a fight. I imagined myself as Mike Tyson, dodging and weaving so as not to get hit. Even the thing that got me into this situation, my football skills, were learned through visualizing the moves I saw when watching Sunday football with my dad every week. Do you see now how imagination can help us go to the fight when we need to confront a predator?

My father told me, "One day, you'll see him again. When you do, your emotions may rage. When you come into contact with a bully, with a predator, with someone who wants to cause you harm, you must remain grounded and calm. You must know that there is a time to engage and a time to retreat. Listen to your body and the answer will come. Never ride the middle line. If you want to engage, go all the way. If you want to retreat, go all the way. Either choice can be the right choice. As men, our ego may tell us to go headfirst into every fight. I am not raising you to live in ego. Sometimes, you will lose. Sometimes, it's not a good fight. Sometimes, it's not a good move. Listen and trust that you will find the answer."

Eventually, I saw my predator, James, again. It was on the same field as our *Killerman* game, but this time we were playing baseball. With my dad's words in my head, I stayed calm and grounded outwardly, even though inwardly I wanted to destroy him.

During the game, my predator walked by me and said, "You're lucky your dad saved you. I was about to work you."

He triggered me to reply, "You're slow, fat, ugly, and can't tackle me. I'm better than you at *Killerman*, and if you want to work me, do it now." I was not afraid of the bully, of the problem, of what could go wrong—it never crossed my mind. I assumed things would work out for me as my father had instructed.

I tossed my baseball glove in the air and got in my stance. I stared into his eyes to see his soul, and I could smell the fear. I looked at his chest to see where all his movements were coming from. I was grounded and calm. My hands were up, I bounced on my toes, and I bobbed my head. This time I was taking the fight to him. I could see the fear in him. What he feared was my preparation. He was unprepared.

A crowd of boys formed around us. James laughed at me like it was a joke. His first throw was a feint; he was just being a cocky bully trying to see if I would back down. But once he threw a punch at me, that was the green light I needed to engage. My father always said, "Do not start fights. Do not start conflict. But if someone threatens you, you have a right to defend yourself."

I hit James with a five-piece combo faster than a fast-food restaurant. He fell to the ground in slow motion; all the boys started screaming in excitement. He got up a few moments later with a bloody nose and ruffled shirt. The time in between this incident and the start of the fight was a blur. Him falling was a blur.

"I'm sorry," James said as he put his hand out in a truce.

I was apprehensive; my hormones were still raging in protective mode. Still, I reluctantly put my hand out. We shook.

He said, "I'm sorry that I attacked you. I lost my cool that day."

I nodded my head in acceptance of his apology.

From that point, life went on. We continued to play baseball. I lived in that town for another year and never encountered a problem with anyone again. Later that summer, James revealed to me that he was getting violently abused at home by his father. While it would take me a few more years to develop and understand true empathy, I felt bad for him. I understand now that he was lashing out at me and creating this external conflict because of the internal conflict created by the violence he faced at home. We were able to put our competitive edges to the side, move forward, and grow in respect for one another. He was a tough kid and wasn't afraid to go toward a fight. I was tough and wasn't afraid of him. I'm confident we both took something from that co-created experience, and now, I assume that we are both trying to show others that we are powerful beyond what we currently think.

Looking back, I'm thankful my predator got whooped on by someone smaller than him because it most likely stopped him going down a path of destruction. I look back at the younger me, and I'm grateful I had a father who knew combat and mindset and was there to protect me when I needed it. I'm grateful that he spoke positive affirmations into my mind about how strong I could be and how wise I could be in the face of conflict and trained me to prepare for the fight.

I believe there are some key takeaways that we can extract and apply to our life as we attack our own predators. This applies even to the 99.9 percent of the things we need to attack that are not physical bullies—things like sugar, waking up on time, making your bed, ignoring your ex, and having that hard boundary conversation with your family members.

# 4 TRAITS TO EMBODY WHEN EMBRACING A MASSIVE CONFLICT

1. *Preparation is the key:* Invest time in training, growth, education, and obtaining experience or knowledge in the field related to your conflict. Preparation rewards the preparer. This means taking an active and engaged approach.

2. *See yourself overcoming:* Your imagination is a powerful tool. Use it to your advantage to sharpen what you believe is possible and to change what is probable. Think big. Think positive. See yourself overcoming. Speak about how great it will be to thrive and win. Call in victory and feel worthy of it as you are putting in work and attention.

3. *Keep it light and fun:* Your journey of overcoming can be fun, light, and joyous. Sometimes we approach things with pure determination and seriousness. You have permission to be determined and serious but to also have fun and enjoy the journey.

4. *Stop being avoidant:* Avoiding prolongs it. Avoiding often makes it worse and makes the problems build. There is something to be said about being patient, about waiting for the right time—yes, we all buy that. However, in your heart, if you are being avoidant and if that avoidance compounds into bigger issues, it's time to hold yourself accountable. It's time to be baptized by the fire.

You will continue to suffer if you have an emotional reaction to everything. True power is sitting back and observing everything with logic. If words control you, that means everyone else can control you; breathe and allow things to pass.

— **Sylvester McNutt III,** *Live the Life You Deserve*

True power is restraint. When you understand your emotions, you understand how to acknowledge them and to allow them to pass. Restraint is checking your actions, reactions, and your overreactions to make sure you are creating the life you deserve.

— **Sylvester McNutt III,** *Live the Life You Deserve*

# TRUE POWER IS RESTRAINT

In the journey of engaging with our conflicts, problems, shadows, and stress, we often overlook the profound strength that lies in restraint. True power is not always about overt aggression or forceful confrontation; it can also be found in exercising self-control and restraint in the face of adversity.

When we think of restraint, we might envision holding back or suppressing our emotions and desires. However, true restraint is a deliberate choice to pause, reflect, and respond consciously instead of reacting impulsively. In the context of fighting our predators, it means thinking about consequences and using our power in the most integrated way possible. You can achieve that safe, integrated energy field we talked about in the previous chapter through building the following skills, which can be seen as different components of restraint.

*Holding Your Frame*

A three-year-old cries when they don't get what they want, and they flop onto the ground. We call it a tantrum, but it's truly a lack of experience, a lack of maturity, and a lack of understanding restraint. No harm, no foul, as we know and expect three-year-olds to act like that. We understand that a three-year-old's brain has not developed the maturity to process all their experiences in what adults would consider a mature way.

As adults, we hold a mature and calming frame to allow children to deal with their conflicts and to assure them that they are safe. We always protect them from those big emotions; however, we still allow them to feel them. Kids need to go through intense experiences to process feelings and develop the maturity to handle them in the future, because it is only when you go to the fight that you learn how to win the battle.

But let's be honest. We all know someone who is 28 years old and acts like a 3-year-old when they don't get what they want. Ha, that is unacceptable—they haven't done the work. This person has not integrated their decades of life into their frame, instead letting themselves be led by every passing emotion. And we all will come across a 16-year-old who has the grounded energy of an elder. We say things to them like, "You have an old soul." We can see that they have begun to integrate restraint into their frame.

### Accountability

We have the power to choose our attitudes, our words, and our behaviors. When we take accountability for our own actions and responses, we become aligned with the life we want to create. Restraint in this way frees us from the grip of external circumstances or provocations. Rather than being driven by the impulses of the moment, we become intentional in our choices.

The black belt who can physically dominate 99.9 percent of the population in a violent situation exercises restraint, wielding their strength with precision only when appropriate. Assume that you are willing to go to the fight and that you have the skills to handle 99.9 percent of all problems. You've leaned in to the work of integration, so you can face the great fights that life will present us with the ease and trust of a black belt in their own power. What would it mean to use this analogy in your own life?

It means you release petty arguments with your partner, and you choose healthy conflict resolution skills. You channel your energy into constructive avenues, enabling you to engage with your conflicts in a more productive and transformative way. You recognize when you are not being accountable for your health, for your dreams, or how you go after the fight in life. You commit to the process of embodying your highest self, to going back to what matters most, which is becoming a master of going to the fight in life. We no longer have time to waste in life. We must go after the fight in the most integrated way possible.

## Detachment

In any situation, we can detach ourselves from the immediate emotional response and gain a broader perspective. Detachment grants us the space and clarity to assess the situation objectively so we can make wiser decisions. When we react impulsively, we often exacerbate conflicts or create unnecessary tension. But when we become observers of our own emotions and thoughts, we recognize that they do not define us. We separate ourselves from the chaos and respond from a place of calm and discernment.

Detachment also plays a pivotal role in resolving conflicts and building harmonious relationships. When we encounter differing opinions or challenging individuals, we can choose to let go of our initial emotional reactions and prejudices. We can listen attentively, suspend judgment, and respond with empathy and compassion. Instead of engaging in heated arguments or escalating tensions, we can find common ground and seek understanding. This fosters an environment of respect, openness, and collaboration, enabling us to forge deeper connections and find mutually beneficial resolutions.

\* \* \*

In our fast-paced, instant-gratification-driven world, cultivating restraint may seem counterintuitive. We are often conditioned to believe that power lies in being loud, forceful, or dominating. However, true power emerges when we exercise restraint and engage with our conflicts from a place of inner strength and calmness. It is in the moments of restraint that we discover our true selves and unleash our highest potential.

To harness the power of restraint, we must cultivate self-awareness and mindfulness. Regular practices such as meditation, journaling, or engaging in introspective exercises can help us develop the ability to observe our thoughts and emotions without being consumed by them. Additionally, learning to regulate our impulses and respond consciously through techniques like deep breathing, visualization, or counting to 10 allows us to pause before reacting impulsively.

As we embrace the practice of restraint, we tap into our inner strength. We increase our ability to respond consciously, thoughtfully, and calmly in the face of conflicts, problems, and stress. Restraint empowers us to navigate life's challenges with wisdom, grace, and integrity.

# JOURNAL PROMPTS:
# 10 MENTAL ANGLES TO REFLECT ON
# WHEN ENGAGING IN CONFLICT

- Reflect on a time in your life when you felt underestimated or faced opposition from others. How did you respond to those challenges? How would you respond now if the current version of you encountered the same conflict?

- How does the concept of "protecting yourself at all times" resonate with you in different aspects of your life, beyond physical confrontations? Is there something you need to do financially, spiritually, emotionally, or even from a mindset perspective to protect yourself at this time in your life?

- How has your perception of "fighting" or conflict evolved over time? How do you navigate the fine line between standing up for yourself and seeking resolutions peacefully? Do you appreciate the way you handle conflict now, or does it need to change? If so, how?

- Do you recall a time where you felt like you were threatened by someone, but it turned out to be a false alarm? What made you view them as a threat initially? What made you realize this person was safe?

- Explore a situation where you had to rely on your instincts and inner voice for guidance. How did you trust yourself in that moment, and what were the outcomes?

- How do you currently view the concept of going after the fight in your own life? Are there areas where you tend to hold back or avoid conflict? How might embracing this idea impact your growth and personal development?

- Is there a conflict you are avoiding because you are not adequate in knowledge or experience to face it? If so, what amount of time of learning or training is required to get there, and when are you going to commit to doing it? (Example: a student who is repeating a failed class for college credits. This student may need to see a tutor and spend an extra four hours in the library per week.)

- What would happen if you went after the fight that you needed to go after? Would you acquire more success, more peace, more happiness?

- If you do not feel strong enough right now to encounter your predator, what community, friends, relationships, or ideas do you need to lean in to?

- Your next level of peace of mind, success, and growth will require you to confront yourself or another person/entity. Are you going to do it, or are you going to stay in the same pattern?

Letting go of who you were is the only way you can become a new person—fall in love with this process of releasing what is no longer in alignment with you so you can make more space and attract what will serve you. You do not owe anything to yesteryear you. That version is gone. Say yes to what you need at this moment. Say yes to fighting for your life, for the life that you deserve, and don't ever feel like you need to apologize for living the life you deserve.

— **Sylvester McNutt III,** *Live the Life You Deserve*

I need everyone to understand this: Once you overcome the darkness that is hurting or haunting you, nothing will ever feel this powerful again. Once you overcome the strain and the pain, the happiness and joy flow effortlessly thereafter. I won't lie to you and say it will be easy, but I will tell you the truth, which is that it will be worth it.

— **Sylvester McNutt III,** *Live the Life You Deserve*

Give yourself permission to be a warrior from time to time. You cannot be passive about your life. There are times where you must step up and fight for your life. Because you can see these words, that time is now. Yes, we do have a desire to create peace and calm internally as well as joy, but we also need to engage in war and conflict at times in life. Sometimes, the only way to feel inner calm is to weather the storm and to fight for your life. I wish I could tell you that life is just cupcakes and rainbows, but it's not. Life will present you with numerous trials and tribulations. You have the power to overcome by tapping into your warrior energy.

— **Sylvester McNutt III,** *Live the Life You Deserve*

Isn't it interesting how we think running from the problem will make the problem go way? And then our avoidance makes it harder and harder to deal with. The ironic thing is a lot of the times we are making the problem bigger in our own heads than it actually is. Attack it today. Deal with it today. Address it so you can move forward.

— **Sylvester McNutt III,** *Live the Life You Deserve*

CHAPTER 5

# SELF-MASTERY: A COMMITMENT TO YOUR UNIQUE SELF

You must connect with what makes you unique, with what calls you, with the things that burn your soul into the history of time. Your exact genetic code has never existed and will never exist again. It is your duty to honor what makes you unique, to honor your gifts, to live the life you deserve. Give yourself permission to make mistakes, for the commitment to self-mastery will require efforts, risks, and making mistakes. Give yourself self-compassion as you get curious about what makes you *you*.

87

Self-mastery is how you show up, how you engage, and how you interact with the world around you and inside of you. This journey is about obtaining the knowledge that will guide you toward a life of thriving. This practice is about knowing your strengths and applying them, and it's about committing to learning how to manage and improve your deficiencies and shortcomings. When it comes to creating the life you want, the life you deserve, you must become a master of yourself.

— **Sylvester McNutt III,** *Live the Life You Deserve*

Honor what is unique about you. Your specific genetic code will never be duplicated. Release the expectations that you need to be what your parents, society, or other people want you to be. You are allowed to be yourself. Honor what makes you unique and you will find a deeper reverence and joy for life.

— **Sylvester McNutt III,** *Live the Life You Deserve*

In this chapter, I'll often use the words *mastery* and *self-mastery*. I want to be clear that self-mastery is about the inner journey while mastery relates to the external journey.

Self-mastery is the practice of becoming an expert on yourself. Mastery is the practice of becoming an expert of a vocation, skill, practice, training, and so on. Self-mastery is a feeling, a state of being that happens through the trial and error of life, through risks, and through learning that helps you on the journey of becoming your highest self. These two concepts work with one another. Your highest self is more imagination based, more of an ideal self, a visual that may not be completely accurate of yourself today. Self-mastery is more literal—it's just an assessment of your inner tool kit.

Self-mastery is how you show up, how you engage, and how you interact with the world around you and inside you. This journey is about obtaining the knowledge that will guide you toward a life of thriving. This practice is about knowing your strengths and applying them, and it's about committing to learning how to manage and improve your deficiencies and shortcomings. When it comes to creating the life you want, the life you deserve, you must become a master of yourself.

Mastery can be used to describe your level of proficiency with a particular skillset, practice, or discipline. For example, Gordon Ramsay is a famous chef. Now, I don't know him as a person, but I'm willing to bet if we asked him, he would say that his level of self-mastery as Gordon is what enabled him to become a master of entertainment, cooking, running businesses, and opening restaurants. Self-mastery, the inner journey, is often the catalyst and lever for mastery, the external journey.

It's true that there are examples of people who have a great deal of mastery to run a business, but they are crumbling inside with drug addiction, depression, impostor syndrome, anxiety, and daily fear. For our journey, however, we are trying to have both self-mastery and the opportunity to commit to a journey of mastery with a skill, talent, vocation, or trade. To do this, let's discuss some of the essential mindsets that will assist us on the journey of self-mastery.

If the goal is to create the life we deserve, then we need to know who we are, what we can do, and how we are showing up.

## EMBODY COMPASSION DURING THE SELF-MASTERY JOURNEY

*Leave guilt at the door.*

*Leave shame at the door.*

*Leave self-judgment at the door, for now.*

*You are a scientist, and your mission is to learn how you are and what you can do.*

Compassion is the emotion of being loving, kind, and safe toward yourself or another. It's about having love and reverence for your human experience. Compassion is not about being weak or pathetic—it's about embodying love, understanding, and treating your body and mind with deep reverence.

Compassion is essential on this journey because the true path of self-mastery is difficult. You will have to break up with old mindsets, and that journey is not easy. You will encounter predators, and those moments will be hard. In life, you will win many great fights, and you will lose some;

both journeys may bring grief and sorrow. Let's be honest: if you are looking to live the life you deserve, that means you will make sacrifices and you will lose and let go of things. That journey of healing requires compassion.

Compassion is a key component of self-mastery. As you venture into mastery of talents, disciplines, skills, and vocations, you must hold reverence for the journey. Most of those journeys are decades and even lifetimes long. There will be a long, dark period in between. There will be impostor syndrome, doubt, and fear—and those emotions are normal. We are not here for toxic positivity, which is where we just focus on the good and ignore the bad and try to "positive energy" our way to where we want to be. Compassion is the way!

Embarking on the path of self-mastery requires more than just dedication and effort; it necessitates treating oneself with kindness and understanding throughout the journey. Self-compassion is necessary as we commit to this journey of mastery because it is about deaths, births, and rebirths. It's about giving ourselves permission to feel the depths of each process. Self-compassion becomes a guiding light, offering solace during challenging times and celebrating accomplishments with genuine joy.

Often we are our harshest critics, quick to judge our missteps and flaws. However, when we cultivate self-compassion, we can transform our inner dialogue into one of encouragement and support—and that is what we need as we commit to mastering the self. Is there a point in the journey where being hard on yourself can serve you? Yes, of course, but at the start it needs to be a commitment to gathering data and allowing yourself to experience things. Fair enough?

## EMBRACING IMPERFECTIONS AS A PART OF BEING HUMAN

Sue Mehrtens, founder of Jungian Center for the Spiritual Sciences, wrote about the Jungian view of perfection:

> There are multiple dangers in a focus on perfection. First is what it can lead to. Because the quest for perfection is a hopeless endeavor, it can become an addiction. Trying to be perfect is a foolproof strategy to foster guilt, shame, self-hatred, and a sense of personal inadequacy. In our patriarchal culture, the notion of perfection as the goal or standard served church leaders well, in terms of keeping control over people, because it encourages feelings of powerlessness and despair. It also breeds fear and anxiety, because of the evaluation and judgment that perfectionism implies. . . .
>
> Perfectionism can warp our imagination. One of our most important human abilities is imagination. Western culture, of course, denigrates this gift (think how many times you have heard, or been told, "Oh, that's just your imagination!"). But our ability to make images, to identify with others, to see ourselves in situations different from the physical reality immediately before us, to cast ourselves into the future and create powerful, attractive visions of what might be—this human power is central to our creativity and to making a better world.[1]

As we pursue our unique journey, we can't do so under the muse of perfection. I am asking for you to embrace the duality of saying yes to compassion and releasing perfection and no to the idea and commitment of keeping perfectionism as a mode of thinking. It doesn't help you. Instead, it blocks play, compassion, and imagination—and those are all elements we need enabled to create the life we deserve.

Scientific studies have revealed the impact of accepting our imperfections on our overall well-being and happiness. Dr. Brené Brown, a renowned researcher on vulnerability and authenticity, has conducted studies highlighting the benefits of embracing imperfections. According to her research, individuals who embrace vulnerability and imperfections tend to lead more fulfilling lives, experience deeper connections with others, and enjoy greater emotional resilience.[2]

Candice Kumai wrote in her book *Kintsugi Wellness*, "Embrace your imperfections; they are the gold that makes you unique."[3] Just as the ancient Japanese art of Kintsugi mends broken pottery with gold, our imperfections enrich the mosaic of our lives, making us whole and more beautiful than ever before.

Remember, self-mastery is the commitment to your unique self. If you are wound up inside fake perfectionism, you will never feel freedom. As you begin to let this go, you become totally free. Perfectionism is not real.

Here is a practical exercise that I have had my clients do. The purpose behind this ritual is to physically identify and then let go and throw away perfectionism.

### *Exercise to Let Go of Perfectionism*

Pull out a piece of paper, 8½ by 11. At the top, write "Letting Go of Perfectionism." On the front side of this paper, freely write everything that you think, know, and feel about perfectionism. Write where it came from. What purpose it serves in your life, if any. If it helps you or hurts you.

Free write.

Then, with a witness, you will destroy this paper in a safe way.

"Destroy" needs to be appropriate and safe for your life. You can rip it, cut it, burn it, or simply toss it in the trash. Again, keep this appropriate for your life and situation. A person who has firepit in their backyard could safely burn this paper in a ceremony, but if you live in an apartment, you may be better off cutting it into pieces—be smart.

## PREPARATION IS THE ULTIMATE TOOL TO ACCESS MASTERY

Alex Honnold's journey as a free solo climber teaches us about both self-mastery and mastery of a skill, passion, or calling. Born on August 17, 1985, in Sacramento, California, Alex developed a love for climbing from a young age. As he honed his skills and grew more adept at the sport, he became particularly drawn to free solo climbing—a form of rock climbing without using ropes, harnesses, or any protective equipment.

One of the most significant milestones in Alex's climbing journey was his audacious goal to free solo El Capitan, a massive granite monolith in Yosemite National Park, California. El Capitan stands approximately 3,000 feet (900 meters) tall and is considered one of the most challenging climbing routes in the world, even when using aid.

He planned to climb the Freerider route, which includes numerous difficult and exposed sections. No one had ever attempted to free solo El Capitan, and the very idea of climbing such a colossal wall without any safety gear was seen as both awe-inspiring and incredibly dangerous.

In 2017, Alex took on the momentous challenge. He spent months meticulously preparing for the ascent, studying every move and sequence, memorizing the route, and practicing on a wall with ropes. Mental preparation was equally vital, as he needed to maintain an unwavering focus and composure to conquer the daunting climb.

Each night after practicing, he would journal on what steps worked and what he didn't like. He would rehearse and memorize the notes in preparation for the following day's attempt. His mental preparation was sharp, like the side of a new set of chef's knives. A big component of his preparation with the notes he took was to imagine himself doing it each day.

As we go through our journeys and commit to mastery, certainly, there will be moments where fear is prevalent. Fear is normal if you have an amygdala that is active. When it came to fear, Alex said, "A lot of people tell you to suppress your fear or get over it. I try to expand my comfort zone by practicing the moves over and over again. I work through the fear until it's not scary anymore."

Over the course of approximately 4 hours and 20 minutes, Alex made history on June 3, 2017, by successfully reaching the summit of El Capitan. His achievement was met with astonishment and admiration from the climbing community and beyond. The feat was documented in the critically acclaimed film *Free Solo*, which showcased the journey leading up to the historic climb and the profound impact it had on Alex's life.[4]

Alex Honnold's journey to free solo El Capitan embodies the essence of self-mastery. It exemplifies the dedication and single-minded pursuit of a dream, pushing the boundaries of human potential. Alex's ability to remain calm under extreme pressure and his willingness to embrace fear with calculated focus is a testament to the immense mental and physical strength required to achieve mastery in any field. By going within and mastering self, he was then able to master this external conquest.

Beyond the accomplishment itself, Alex's journey inspires others to challenge conventional limits, to believe in the power of relentless preparation, and to trust in their abilities.

## MINDSET NEEDED FOR MASTERY

One of my favorite basketball players of all time, Kobe Bryant, had what I believe to be one of the best and ideal mental approaches to preparation. In his TEDxShanghai-Salon talk, "Power of the Mind," he says: "If your job is to try to be the best basketball player you can be, to do that you have to practice and you have to train. You want to train as much as you can as often as you can. . . . It makes sense to get up and start your day early because you can get more work in. . . . If I start earlier, then I can train more hours, and I know the other guys aren't doing it because I know what their training schedule is. So I know if I do this consistently over time, the gap is going to widen. . . . My first class in high school was at 7:45, I used to get to the gym around 5 A.M., and I'd play before school. . . . My coach would show up and we'd do all these basketball drills. Just me and my coach, and sometimes it would just be me and the janitor. . . . I would play during lunch and then practice after. Then go home, do my schoolwork, and then watch a bunch of game film and games on TV and study film. . . ." He sums up the mindset behind all this preparation: "To me, the mentality is a really simple one in the sense that the confidence comes from preparation. When the game's on the line, I'm not asking myself to do something I haven't done thousands of times before."[5]

Tom Cruise said, "I'm up at 4 or 5 A.M. every morning. . . . I really enjoy working hard. I work seven days a week. Being on a movie set is a holiday for me, I rarely take vacations. Life is about learning new things. It's about challenging yourself."[6] Tom Cruise is one of the best actors of all time, and his commitment to mastery is what created this path. I loved this quote, especially the part about work feeling like a vacation. He built a life that feels like a vacation because he listened to his calling. He got to know his true self, and that person needs to work on movies.

In an inspiring commencement speech at Dillard University, Denzel Washington said, "Don't be afraid to think outside the box. Don't be afraid to fail big, to dream big, but remember dreams without goals are just dreams and they ultimately fuel disappointment. So have dreams, but have goals. . . . Simple goals, but have goals and understand that to achieve these goals you must apply discipline and consistency. . . . You have to work at it. Every day you have to plan—every day. You've heard the saying that we don't plan to fail, we fail to plan. Hard work works. Working really hard is what successful people do. . . . Remember that just because you're doing a lot more doesn't mean you're getting a lot more done. Don't confuse movement with progress. My mom told me you can run in place all the time and never get anywhere. Continue to strive, continue to have goals, continue to progress."[7]

For over 20 years, I have practiced writing every single day. I did that before I had a website, before social media even existed, and before anyone ever knew about my skill. I wrote every day as it was something deep inside of me that was calling me. I would fill up notebook after notebook, obsessed with practicing the art of writing. I was on my journey of both self-mastery, the inner path, and mastery of words, the external path.

When I took a poetry writing class in college, my professor, who was a published author, told me in front of everyone, "Sylvester, your work just doesn't connect on an emotional level yet. You have to get better."

When I received that feedback, I said to myself, "One day, I will be a best-selling author. I will stay committed to getting better. My day is coming—believe me." (I used the laws of attraction and deliberate creation here, which I will explain in the next chapter, along with how you can integrate them into your life.)

My professor was right. At 18, I wasn't a master yet. I was still learning, but I was committed. I'm grateful my professor didn't baby me. She didn't pacify me. She didn't give me praise because I didn't deserve that. She was hard on me and demanded more; she demanded that I honor the practice with my effort and attention.

Along the journey of mastery, there will be a teacher or mentor who will challenge you, teach you, and mold you. It won't always come as a pat on the back or an attaboy. Some are looking for easy cupcakes and rainbows to illuminate the path. Your mastery journey is going to be hard—embrace it now. Nothing easy will come to you. And the people who tell you that you're not good enough are not haters most of the time. If they have done it, they are being honest; they can see that you aren't at the level you need to be at.

Every single day of my life, I feel like giving 140 percent to my passions, to my craft, to my healing, to my purpose, and to mastery both within myself and for whatever external journeys that I am on at the time . . . I don't have days to waste.

You don't have time to waste.

You don't have days to waste.

After decades of writing, I put together a book. The second after that was finished, I started working on the next one, and then I did it again. I did this process over and over and over. Once you read this book, understand that I am already working on the next book. That does not come from the emotion of lack or not being good enough; it comes from the curious pursuit of following my own self-mastery journey. It comes from the commitment to honoring the gifts and privileges that have been bestowed upon me.

You must honor the gifts that you have been given and honor the gifts that are screaming at you to cultivate. A big question that comes up for many is how to recognize or honor the gifts that we have. Simple: you listen and go within.

Societies that are rooted in capitalism make us think about making money at the forefront of our brains. And yes, we do need income, savings, and investments on a practical level. Notice that when I shared quotes from people who inspired me, the underlying theme was a calling, a curiosity, a passion. You see that in my testimony about writing. It's not about money and the external path. It's about an inward path. In each situation, money was a consequence and not the motivation.

Your calling does not have to be a job. Mastery in the external form does not have to be something you make money with. Each year around Halloween, my neighbor turns his mansion into the biggest creepy-crawly fun fest you've ever seen. This guy has lasers, a full graveyard, a smoke show, and songs playing. He hires real human actors; he has paintings and spiders bigger than a Hummer truck. He makes zero dollars from this. He does it because this type of creativity calls him, making him feel whole and giving him something to chase.

## YOUR MINDSET AND ENERGY WILL CARRY YOU THROUGH OPPORTUNITIES AS YOU CHANGE IN LIFE

Mindset and energy are *everything* in cultivating the life we deserve. Way back in the day, when my gift and opportunity was football, I knew I wasn't the fastest, biggest, or strongest, so I had to sharpen myself in other ways. Self-mastery during that journey meant I had to be the smartest player on the field since I was not as athletically gifted as everyone else. I would go to the gym in the morning to lift weights before school. I used to read books from the 1950s and 1960s about what successful football players had done and how they approached the game. During lunch breaks, I would watch game film and study tendencies of this week's appointment. I wanted to get any mental edge I could and sacrificed the social hour of lunch so I could sharpen my mind—it was lonely. Watching film gives you a mental edge and advantage during the games. Your mind goes into a place of *imagination,* and the games slow down.

The same intensity to self-mastery is what I applied when I was working in corporate America and I knew there was a book in me. The book was screaming at me. I would do the best I could at my job. Daily, I was dedicated, I was the best in my role and my numbers showed it, and my energy was contagious to my staff. But my calling would not silence itself, and so I had to respect and honor the job I had while also honoring what my soul was asking of me.

I would excuse myself from the sales floor, go into the bathroom, lock the door, and lean on the wall. I would open the Notes app on my phone and write as much as I could in a 5- to 10-minute window. I would completely black out the world and give everything I could to that writing session. And when I couldn't break away, I would memorize what I wanted to write. I would say the words over and over, forcing myself to memorize the lines. I would do this every hour at my eight-hour job. This gave me at least one hour of writing during the day, even though I had a full-time job. I felt no guilt about excusing myself to work on my book once I saw how my co-workers threw away their spare time, also taking extra breaks to smoke and chat, and none of them thrived at the job like I did.

I needed that job and couldn't quit until I saved up $30,000. I told myself that once I saved up that much, I could quit and chase my passion and become a full-time author. I told myself that I could live "broke" on one meal a day, never travel, and not buy anything. I was committed to minimalism: not drinking, not going out, and not dating. Pared down to the essentials of rent and food and such, I could keep my annual budget below $10,000, so I knew I could live like that for at least three years. When I made that declaration that I was going to pursue being an author full-time, something changed. My path to self-mastery and external mastery got easier. I had three years to make this happen, or I had to give up.

During that era, I knew that I needed to keep a sharp mind, so I trained my body every single day. I went to the gym seven days a week at 5 or 6 A.M. Even if I needed rest, I would go to the gym anyway and lay on a mat and nap. Then when I woke up, I'd get to my workout. I did that several times to honor my commitment and so I wouldn't stay in bed and slack off.

For three years, all I did was train, write, walk to the grocery store, and make whole foods and slow meals. During that time, my car was repossessed. I couldn't afford the $421 monthly payments, so my options were to buy a bike or walk. My value system changed when that happened because it made me realize that this country is built on extracting money from you. I decided to get my expenses even lower so I could focus on self-mastery.

My mission to self-mastery didn't care about what job I had. My mission to self-mastery couldn't care less what excuse I could've grabbed. When I first started writing, I committed to writing 2,000 words per day, and I did that for almost 10 full years. I'm willing to bet my next meal that the practice of writing 2,000 words per day for a decade is what helped me achieve this skill, confidence, and energy.

Self-mastery requires you to go within. It requires you to honor what you hear, what you feel, what is calling you. This is an intuitive journey. Self-mastery is often connected to external pursuits and destinations. There is an enmeshment there.

## FINDING PURPOSE IN YOUR VOCATION

In Robert Greene's book, *Mastery*, he talks about the value of doing a job that you love, a job that aligns with your passion. In the book, he describes each of us as having a calling, a "Life's Task," which is what we are meant to accomplish in our life. Robert says, "At your birth a seed is planted. That seed is your uniqueness. It wants to grow, transform itself, and flower to its full potential. It has a natural, assertive energy to it. Your Life's Task is to bring that seed to flower, to express your uniqueness through your work. You have a destiny to fulfill. The stronger you feel and maintain it—as a force, a voice, or in whatever form—the greater your chance for fulfilling this Life's Task and achieving mastery."[8]

Robert Greene describes three stages through which we realize our Life's Task, and I share my take on them here.[9]

### *Stage 1: Connect or Reconnect with Your Inclinations*

Looking inward is always the first step in any transformation, desired lifestyle, or personal development change that you seek. Looking inward allows you to listen to the deepest inclinations that are occurring inside you. Modern society is great at creating noise and distractions. Reading a book that invites you inward is great, but there's still more work you can do, like listening to your desires, tuning in to your breath, and truly asking yourself, "What do I want?"

Look for a core to your character, and that is how you "find yourself." It's possible that when you were a teenager, you were into sports and the solar system. Now, as an adult, you work a job where you feel "lost" or "trapped" or like you are wasting time. It's time to listen to that inclination that is calling you back. Maybe the call is to science or to sports, and you transition back to those industries, somehow.

### *Stage 2: Enlarge Your Perception of Work*

Enlarging the perception of your work holds immense power in your pursuit of mastery. Many people unconsciously operate in two separate spheres: work and real life. Work is considered just a means to an end, a way to support your real life, which is where you find pleasure and fulfillment. Instead, you can see work as part of your life and calling and a way to connect with your authentic self.

### Stage 3: See Your Career or Vocational Path as a Journey with Twists and Turns Rather than a Straight Line

When you embrace your career as a journey filled with twists and turns rather than viewing it as a linear path, you open yourself up to diverse experiences and learning opportunities. This expansion not only fosters neuroplasticity, enhancing your cognitive abilities, but also enables cross-domain knowledge transfer, leading to innovative problem-solving and a broader perspective. By allowing yourself to explore and connect with different fields, you unleash your creativity, resilience, and adaptability, all vital traits for achieving true mastery.

## LOOKING DEEPER INTO VOCATION AS A PATH TO MASTERY

*Vocation* means to call. The meaning of the word originated in Christianity, as people often referred to hearing a voice of God and obeying that call.[10] The journey of self-mastery can unfold through many different verticals in life. We can commit to different activities, identities, and experiences.

Our society is vastly different than the ones that have come before us, and of course, the future will look different than what we see today. Humans mostly are finding ways to make things better, easier, or more efficient—or so we think. As we know, these efforts produce great results that have negative and positive impacts on human experience as we know it. Regardless of how society changes, what we need will always be the same.

The hierarchy of needs, a theory postulated by psychologist Abraham Maslow, designed a blueprint for us to understand the motivations behind behavior based on need. He describes five levels, with the lowest level being the most basic needs for survival, our physiological needs, then safety and security, love and belonging, self-esteem, and finally self-actualization. We can only move on to addressing higher-level needs when our basic needs are fulfilled.

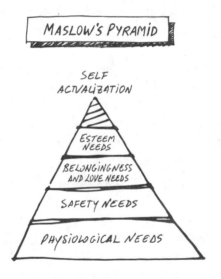

When we think of self-mastery as an inner journey or as it relates to a vocation, perhaps we could accept that the journey plays directly into our human needs. Taking the example that I just shared of writing mastery, we could observe that I wanted to pursue being a writer because it touches several needs. We could say that it gave me self-esteem, it helped me self-actualize, and perhaps it brought me love and a sense of belonging. We could argue that once I did finally get income from that pursuit, it brought a satisfaction to physiological needs. When we occupy our life with activities, tasks, vocations, and community that can fulfill multiple spaces in the pyramid of our hierarchy of needs, we feel more purpose, belonging, and meaning, and we feel more alive.

When I was a young boy, my class went on a field trip to a farm in southern Illinois. There, I met an inspiring woman whose testimony about vocation, work, and mastery registered with me, but I never fully understood what she was saying until I was older, had some experience, and had found myself.

On the farm, we spent the entire day playing with and feeding chickens, picking apples, and making cider. We milked cows, churned butter, and made biscuits. We were able to see how honey was made, and yes, we were able to put butter and honey on our biscuits, which is an elite experience. We didn't get to see the hunt or how the animals were butchered and treated. However, I imagine that would be available for the older kids. We chopped down trees, flipped soil over, and learned how to plant crops as well. This was easily the best field trip I'd ever been on.

I'm a city boy through and through, having grown up in a small apartment in Chicago. I'd never been exposed to the rural lifestyle, but this trip gave me an internal expansion. It was this trip that helped me contextualize the luxuries that I had access to—even though we weren't rich, we still had the ability to go to the grocery store and buy a wide array of food. We had access to big roads, big schools, and lots of entertainment.

On the farm, I wondered aloud, "Do you ever get bored here since you don't have video games, arcades, and big malls like we have in the city?"

Everyone working on the farm that day chuckled. It's a fair question that a city kid might ponder. Mrs. Tompkins, an older woman full of grace and with a big smile and perfectly braided red hair, said, "Thank you for your question. There's plenty to do here. There's plenty to learn and lots of growing to do. We find purpose in this work and in our community. We find purpose in being connected to the land and having a giving relationship where we also receive. We sleep well each night knowing that we give our day to the earth and to each other. We wake up each day ready to nourish ourselves with activities that are meaningful to us, to the family that came before us, and to the families that we are raising."

Younger me didn't fully appreciate what she said because I didn't have context to grasp all the nuance. However, to a degree, I understood what she was saying, and I continued reflecting on it over the years.

Her "job" was to do soul work, work that meant something to her on a soul level and that inspired her to master herself (self-mastery) and the skills needed to be on the farm (mastery). She woke up every day and did work that made her feel alive, valued, and connected to those she loved most. She had reached mastery within because she honored and listened to what she needed. She reached mastery as a host because she created memorable experiences that quite literally lasted a lifetime for some of us. Mrs. Tompkins was able to find purpose, connection, and love through her vocation.

## DIFFERENT PATHS OF MASTERY

Can you find mastery outside a career? Yes, of course.

The modern society that we live in is based on capitalism. Consequently, it has been driven into our psyche that who we are is our job, what we need to pursue is job related, and we are better humans when we make and have a lot of money. The purpose of capitalism is to drive profits, to maximize wealth, and to condition us to be good workers.

Think about it. One of the questions people ask children is, "What do you want to be when you grow up?" Now, I can't assume why people ask that. I can't assume that they have read this book and are asking the kid what calling is inside of them. I can't say with a lot of confidence that people are asking about what type of values or integrity the kid wants to possess. It would appear to me that they are asking: What type of job do you want? The social conditioning starts young.

But here's the truth: we all have different paths. And when it comes to career and vocation, some of us will find ourselves in a job related to passions and things that make us feel something deeper. But some of us won't. Some of us will do jobs we are okay with, jobs we are average at and that help us take care of bills since we are born into a society that requires us to pay for things to survive.

I'm of the frame of mind that for me, yes, I desire a certain level of wealth since I own a company and have a family. So yes, I like capitalism for what it has provided me. But I don't love all the consequences and tenets that come with it.

On a deeper emotional and soul level, I understand and accept that some people couldn't care less. I am not here to call those people less than or unworthy of living the life they deserve. If you truly don't care about finding yourself in your vocation, I understand why. If that's how you feel, you can build your life around your hobbies and get a job that supports you. That means you must find jobs that set you up so you have the agency, time, and resources to invest in your interests. I know a guy who left his legal career in the United States and moved to Costa Rica so he could surf daily. He was able to work at a local coffee shop there, and for him, that is living the life he deserves. Anything is possible.

Living the life you deserve is an authentic journey, and you have permission to manifest it in any way that's true to you.

If you feel like you don't know what your purpose is, then this is a time to be curious, ask questions, and try a bunch of things. You don't need to "know" what is next when you are in a deep phase of curiosity and exploration. If you're not sure whether you even have a purpose, know this: a sense of purposelessness is not real. You are simply distracted, putting your focus on activities and energy fields that do not serve your soul. Have compassion for who you are and where you are. This is your invitation to pay attention to what makes you alive, to what tingles your soul, to what makes you engage in life. It's time to play and to be curious.

Honor what is unique about you. Your specific genetic code will never be duplicated. Release the expectations that you need to be what your parents, society, or other people want you to be. You are allowed to be yourself. Honor what makes you unique, and you will find a deeper reverence and joy for life.

Focus on what is possible. When we attempt to make big changes in our lives, we can feel fear and have impostor syndrome. It's okay to lack confidence at the start of the journey because confidence comes from proof. This is new. You don't have proof yet, so instead of looking for confidence, speak life into yourself and simply affirm, "It's possible. I can do this, and it's possible."

# JOURNAL PROMPTS: MASTERY AND SELF-MASTERY

- Finding yourself requires you to take risks. This means there will be mistakes. Are you going to give yourself permission to make mistakes? Self-mastery or mastery of a task requires the ability to get through mistakes.

- When you hear "commitment to your unique self" what comes up for you? I enjoy writing and working out. Those things make me feel unique. I give myself permission to honor what makes me who I am. Have you made the commitment to your unique self? If you have not, what does starting today look like for you?

- Mastery of a skill can make us feel alive, like we belong, and even like we have purpose. Where are you with this journey? If you are not where you want to be, what curiosity is calling you?

- Self-mastery means to know yourself. What is your perspective on strengths versus weaknesses? Let's say both are important and that sometimes you need to focus on one more than the other. What season are you currently in? Is this the season to focus on what is weak about you and get better? Is this the season to focus on your gifts, what is going well and to grow that? Yes, sure you could do both at the same time, or you could focus on one. What season are you in currently?

As you fall deeper in love with this version of who you are, I challenge you to commit to what makes you unique. We lead ourselves astray when we dismiss and devalue what makes us special. At the core, sure, we are all human, and we are all unique in some way. Your exact genetic code will never exist again. Therefore, it is your duty to recognize your gifts, talents, and life's paths so you can honor them daily.

— **Sylvester McNutt III,** *Live the Life You Deserve*

I need you to understand this: humans will always search for purpose. "Purpose" changes throughout a lifetime. What gave you purpose 20 years ago may be boring and mundane today. If you are on a search for a new "purpose," then open yourself up because it can be found in a hobby, a trade, or an activity; it can be found in the most random places. Open your heart to the possibility that purpose may find you in a package that looks different than what you know today.

— **Sylvester McNutt III,** *Live the Life You Deserve*

You will go on a pursuit at one point or another in your life. It may be inner as you expand yourself spiritually or emotionally. It may be external as you seek a particular career or look to arrive at a certain point in life. Make me one promise, though, along the way. Promise me you will give your best efforts the most energy and be absolutely dedicated to the journey. Promise me that you will commit and overcommit. Promise me that you will prove to yourself what you are capable of. I am not focused on the result. I am only asking you to form an energy and mindset perspective that you stay focused and aligned and pursue this thing you want like it is the only thing that matters.

— **Sylvester McNutt III,** *Live the Life You Deserve*

You must know yourself to go to the next level that is calling you. You can lie to friends, family, and social media, but you cannot lie to yourself. Know yourself and your weaknesses if you want to get through this next threshold. Everything depends on your ability to be honest with what you have and do not have. Most will lie, but not you. You will be authentic, and you will focus on getting to know the real you.

— **Sylvester McNutt III**, *Live the Life You Deserve*

You owe yourself an apology for playing small before. You owe yourself an apology for the things you let slide. You owe yourself an apology for what you used to settle for. It's your time to step into your power, into this new version of you.

— **Sylvester McNutt III**, *Live the Life You Deserve*

## CHAPTER 6

# HOW TO DELIBERATELY DESIGN THE LIFE YOU DESERVE

B e a deliberate creator in your life. Be mindful of the language you choose as you design your life. The science of deliberate creation says that how you think and speak creates an energy field within your actions and around your space—so be mindful of how you speak. When you accept the laws of attraction and deliberate creation, you accept accountability for your life. You accept that you design and create your life with your actions, mindsets, and environment. Leaning in to your unique self empowers you to design the life that you were meant to lead.

Most things in life come down to what you feel about yourself. Change your feelings and you change your life. Change how you perceive particular feelings and you will change your life even more.

— **Sylvester McNutt III,** *Live the Life You Deserve*

If you are young—dream big. If you are old—dream big. You are never too late and never too early. This is your life, and you have permission to live fully, to give everything you have. Keep dreaming!

— **Sylvester McNutt III,** *Live the Life You Deserve*

The words you speak have power and consequences. Words compose our language, and our language structures our interpretation of the world, how we tell our story, and how we express ourselves. Everyday life revolves around speaking, writing, reading, and listening to language. We can gain a deeper insight into who we are by observing and auditing the words we use. We can gain information by listening to how others tell their stories and as they communicate their pain or joys.

When I look back on my life, I have a deep reverence for my time working in corporate America because it taught me how to become aware of my language, how I was speaking, and what I was saying to myself about what was possible. After I finished playing arena football, I was thriving in my career at Verizon Wireless, first as a sales rep, then as an assistant manager and a store manager. When I was 23, I was on the fast track to become a director in my early 30s and to become an area president by my late 30s. Working my way up the corporate ladder was a given; I was next in line every year of my career there. With my passion for impacting people, I was confident that path was to become one of the most important corporate leaders. I was going to lead people with empathy, humor, and an immense amount of inspiration and motivation.

While I was grateful for the substantial income my job provided, especially at such a young age, I didn't feel an attachment to the actual work. It began to drain me, and my soul felt truly empty because it didn't touch what made me unique. As a consequence, I found myself caught between two opposing forces: the need to take care of myself by working at a great job that I didn't love and the desperate longing for fulfillment. The job was fulfilling the basic level of physiological needs on Maslow's pyramid, but my soul was yearning for self-actualization. One could also say that this conflict I faced was a predator, and in order for me to conquer it, I had to go on the journey of preparing for the great fight. Little did I know that this internal battle taking over my mind was also leading me closer to listening to my own truth.

In the break room at Verizon Wireless, surrounded by the noise of ringing phones and bustling employees, I first listened to the audiobook of *The Law of Attraction* by Esther and Jerry Hicks. Something within me started to stir. It was as if a whisper of truth was seeping through the cracks of my seemingly perfect corporate life, reaching the Texas-size hole within my soul.

At first, I had a deep resistance to how they presented the material. Esther channels messages from Source energy through a collective of beings known as Abraham. It seemed gimmicky at first, but I gave it a listen, and I am so grateful that I kept an open mind.

Looking back, the connections between my path and Abraham-Hicks's sends chills up and down my body. Yes, I eventually became a Hay House author, just as they were. They too discovered this voice, this Source, and this energy while they were in Phoenix, Arizona. When I relocated to Phoenix from Chicago, it was not just for my corporate job but also for healing, to find myself, and to connect to my spirituality. Phoenix is where I began to feel a deeper connection to life. Later, I would also have my own experiences with channeling Source for others and myself to gain insight to a deeper wisdom.

The fact that all this lines up and now I have the ability to look back and publish a book with Hay House lets me know 100 percent that the law of attraction and the science of deliberate creation are real, and these universal laws are some of the most important aspects of living the life we deserve.

As I listened to *The Law of Attraction* audiobook, I heard Esther say, "We want you to understand the magnificence of your Being, and we want you to understand who-you-really-are and why you have come forth into this physical dimension."[1] I felt a lightning bolt shimmy through my spine. It felt like Source was speaking directly to me and through me. I understand that other authors may have varying definitions of Source. For me, it's truly an intrinsic connection to God or the Universe or whatever you want to call it. It's a connection to soul energy or some power that I can't explain but I can feel.

Esther described the three Universal Laws:

- *The Law of Attraction:* "That which is like unto itself, is drawn."

- *The Science of Deliberate Creation:* "That which I give thought to and that which I believe or expect—is."

- *The Art of Allowing:* "I am that which I am, and I am willing to allow all others to be that which they are."[2]

Esther's words felt like they were taking over my soul as she said, "The more you come to understand the power of the Law of Attraction, the more interest you will have in deliberately directing your thoughts—for you get what you think about, whether you want it or not. Without exception, that which you give thought to is that which you begin to invite into your experience."[3]

I interpret the law of attraction as "like attracts like." I see it as a simple understanding that you will bring more into your life of what you think *is* and what you think *will be.* Whatever you want, you need to be a home for. This is why it is important that you are mindful of the thoughts you give power, of what you say, and what you repeat. You can use your thoughts to change your energy and perspective. As Esther described it, "When you *feel* prosperous, you will attract circumstances of prosperity. When you *feel* loved, you will attract circumstances of love. *Literally, the way you feel is your point of attraction*."[4]

Most things in life come down to what you feel about yourself. Change your feelings, and you change your life. Change how you perceive particular feelings, and you will change your life even more.

As I became more attuned to the law of attraction, I inspected the quality of my thoughts. That is when I knew my time at this job was about to end. At that moment I knew a death was going to occur—when I went to engage this predator lurking in the shadows.

## BE A DELIBERATE CREATOR OF THE LIFE YOU DESERVE

I left work that day so inspired. I went home mumbling over and over, "I am a best-selling author. The world wants to read my stories. I am a best-selling author. The world wants to hear my ideas. I am a best-selling author. I write with love and compassion. I am a best-selling author, and I love my job." I did that because I knew in my heart that I wanted to find a way to become an author. That childhood inclination was always present for me.

I was in a trance driving home, repeating those affirmations over and over. I don't recall eating that night. I don't recall getting in bed and going to sleep. I do remember going home and opening my laptop after work. I started working on a book; I wrote for hours. The next day, I did the same thing—I wrote for hours. The next day, it got worse (in a good way). I sat on the bathroom floor at work, writing stories, poems, and ideas on my cellphone. I wrote almost every waking second. I was obsessed. I was in the trance of the law of attraction.

In that transformative moment, I realized that I couldn't sacrifice my self-actualization desires any longer. As I began to honor my inner voice and put energy into my passion of writing, I found that the fight with this predator became easier. No amount of success in the corporate world could fill the void left by neglecting my passions. I knew I had to act and face this yearning within me head-on. The commitment to write happened shortly after I confronted what was happening within gave me access to that hole. It didn't feel like a hole anymore—it felt like the pathway to gold, to joy, to the elixir of my life. *(Tap, tap, click—save work.)*

After two months I released my first book, *The Accelerated: Success Is a Choice*, on Amazon. In that book I literally wrote the exact mindset I had to become so successful at that age and the exact mindset I would use to become successful with the rest of my career. If you've ever made a song, danced, meditated, played a sport, or committed yourself to making an amazing meal, then you can relate to this experience of channeling Source.

Writing a book is an experience of channeling Source, as the majority of what you write is coming from your subconscious. You are channeling your shadow, your deepest wounds, your deepest gifts and wisdom. When that obsession began, I didn't even feel like I was there. I felt almost like a vessel.

"For the rest of my time, I will tell people that I am a best-selling author." I said this to myself once I was done writing the book—even though nobody had bought my first book. I had no team, no marketing, and no push behind me. Nevertheless, writing this book was necessary; it was an initiation process. It was the death of the old me who didn't have the vision, and it was the birth of the new me that knew what was possible, the version of me who embraced the law of attraction. It was not a time to measure success through sales, reach, and impact. Many times on our journey, we look too soon for external markers of success when what is most important is embodiment and being in the moment.

Abolish all the mindsets, phrases, and words that keep you out of the life you want to live. You must speak about what you want as if it has *already* happened. If that process feels disingenuous for you, speak about it as if it is *going to* happen—you must. When pondering the dreams you want to create, you must use your passion and deep emotion to *feel* it in your body, to feel the emotions of the experience, even though it hasn't unfolded yet.

When I was driving home from work that day, I was channeling Source and creating my future: "I am a best-selling author. The world wants to read my stories. I am a best-selling author. The world wants to read my ideas. I am a best-selling-author. I write with love and compassion. I am a best-selling author, and I love my job."

Many people misunderstand and disrespect the laws of attraction and deliberate creation, and then they have cognitive dissonance wondering why they have created a situation that wasn't what they wanted. Esther Hicks beautifully describes the law of deliberate creation: "That which I give thought to and that which I believe or expect—is. In short, you get what you are thinking about, whether you want it or not."[5]

You can attract only what you feel you are deserving of. We often wonder why we are in a situation that is nowhere near what we desired, and it's simply because we didn't surrender to the desire; we didn't allow it to take us over. If there is a present desire, idea, or something major that is brewing, surrender to it. Lean in to it; allow it to grow.

Never stop dreaming and believing in what you can do. Anything is possible with the right mindset, consistent work ethic, and a hunger for knowledge. Commit yourself to the actions and environment that will create the result you want. Dream big, think big, and take action daily.

If you are young—dream big. If you are old—dream big. You are never too late and never too early. This is your life, and you have permission to live fully, to give everything you have. Keep dreaming!

## ALIGNMENT AND EMBODYING THE OUTCOME

Friend, you must fully embody the outcome you want by believing in it now as you align and work to create it. This is why we were talking about facing the predator; this is why we talked about preparing for and engaging in the great fight—for many of us, there may be emotional blockages present on our journeys, like fear, shame, or guilt. This season of our life where we go to the fight, where we go to the conflict and lean in, is where we develop and garner the strength and belief that will helps us arrive at the point we are looking to reach.

This arc of the hero's journey exists so we can experience something meaningful, so we can accept and honor the invitation that life has given us and step into the life we deserve. In every story, the protagonist is faced with both inner and external conflict. Once the heroine finds out what she needs to conquer within, that gives her the confidence and power level to overcome what she wants to conquer externally. The law of attraction will help you with this: believe you can do it, see yourself doing it, and align with the environments that will assist you.

In his wonderful book *Breaking the Habit of Being Yourself*, Joe Dispenza talks about creating a state of being by being conscious of how you think and how you feel. The law of attraction works due to the same principle that applies to atoms—like attracts like. The energy of your thoughts is attracted to energies of objects that share the same energy. He writes, "Quantum creating only works when your thoughts and feelings are aligned. . . . When you hold clear, focused thoughts about your purpose, accompanied by your passionate emotional engagement, you broadcast a stronger electromagnetic signal that pulls you toward a potential reality that matches what you want."[6]

We can use the law of attraction + imagination today to guide us. As you get in your journal tonight after reading this chapter, I want you to close your eyes and see the reality you are looking to create. If you are in high school and you want to play on a sports team and attend university, you can. See yourself wearing the jersey. Hear your name being called on the loudspeaker and feel yourself in the dugout, on the field, or in the starting blocks. See yourself eating the team meal a few hours before the game. Close your eyes and feel the grass and dirt that will be on your hands. Imagine the sweat dripping down your forehead and see yourself wiping it away. Look up at the scoreboard and see that there's less than 10 seconds left for your team to score. Just like a little kid, imagine yourself hitting the game-winning shot. And then burst into a moment of joy as you feel your teammates jump on you. Laugh and smile with confidence knowing that you trained for this for 25,000 hours. See yourself talking to the local reporter as you get ready to share your testimony about how you beat your rival, how you became the hero. They'll ask you what went through your head as you were taking the shot, and your answer will be simple: "When I was younger, I imagined this situation happening. I've seen this play out in my head before, and it has in practice all the time. I knew it going in. I was ready for this."

Maybe, you're not an athlete anymore. Maybe you're stuck at a job you hate. You work because it pays the bills, but it's a soulless and thankless task. Every single day when you clock out, you feel relieved; pressure and stress have been taken off your shoulders. However, the job took so much from you that you don't have much to give to all things relational anymore. The relationship with self is weak. If you have a partner, you look at them as a burden. If you have kids, you love them, but they feel like a pit of draining energy. And this situation might be why you drink alcohol or why you have raging anger inside of you. I promise there is a way out—and it's through alignment with a deep intention, strong emotion, and visualizing what you want to feel.

You love your kids, but you need better boundaries with them. See yourself as a parent who sets healthy boundaries. Healthy relationships need boundaries; it's that simple. And if you don't show your kids how to set boundaries, then who will?

The only reason you resent your spouse and are angry with them is because you don't get the quality time with them that you once had. See yourself as a couple who travels again, as a couple who goes on dates. You can wear your fancy clothes or whatever makes you both feel attractive.

And the job, yes, if you cannot change it, then the only thing to change is your mindset. You shift your mindset to be positive, to be grateful. You stop complaining about your boss. Yes, I know, you feel like your boss is beneath you and that you could do their job—you're right, and that means it's time for you to take your career more seriously and get promoted. A promotion may occur at this company, or it may occur at another, or it may occur through creating your own business. Yes, if you are not happy there, then you first are going to change your mindset to do everything you can there, *then* you are going to put in hundreds of applications in jobs across the entire world. Yes, the world—think bigger than your neighborhood. And you're not doing this to complain, to be a negative Nancy, or to run from the problems. This is a full-on assault of the problems, but you're now doing it with aligned and focused energy, with a strong intention, and with powerful intentions behind it. When you apply for these jobs, you will see yourself getting the position you deserve, getting the pay you want, and working with a team that has empathy and love.

Being a deliberate creator is often an emotional experience. It can be created from positive emotions like joy, happiness, and pride. It can also occur from negative emotions like fear, guilt, and shame. Creation can come from any of those emotions, and it can flow from conscious or unconscious thoughts, or thoughts big or small. The combinations are endless, and it's a tool we can use right now as we design the life we deserve.

> *The person who says, "I will never be able to pay my bills," is just as much of a creator as the person who says "I deserve abundance." Choose wisely.*

You are a deliberate creator of your life. You design your life with your thoughts and actions. Keep these reminders with you as you ride the wave of deliberate creation:

Effective immediately, it's time to commit to training your mind and body for the outcomes you want to feel. You must be in the best shape of your life in the heart, mind, and body. Your big dreams will require a lot of effort, energy, and aligned actions to manifest them. Take good care of yourself so you can take the actions needed to create the life you deserve.

— **Sylvester McNutt III,** *Live the Life You Deserve*

Become the deliberate creator of your life by mindfully designing your thoughts and speaking them into existence. Your words hold the power to shape your reality, so speak in a hopeful and positive way about what you can do, what is possible, and why things will work out in the best way. Embody your dreams with unwavering belief and passionate emotion to manifest them.

— **Sylvester McNutt III,** *Live the Life You Deserve*

Listen closely to the whispers of truth that seep through the cracks of your seemingly perfect life. They hold the keys to unlocking your deepest desires and fulfilling your purpose. The perfect life that we all pretend to have is a façade, a mask, and none of us are happy wearing these fake faces. Commit to your authenticity, to being yourself, to finding joy and happiness within your story and in your mind.

— **Sylvester McNutt III,** *Live the Life You Deserve*

Don't sacrifice your innermost desires for the sake of societal expectations. Embrace the transformative journey of pursuing your passions and witness the birth of a new and fulfilled version of yourself. Channel your inner desires and become a magnet for the reality you seek.

— **Sylvester McNutt III,** *Live the Life You Deserve*

Release the mindsets and words that limit you from living your desired life. Instead, align your thoughts, feelings, and actions to become a quantum creator of your reality. Speak with intention, and visualize your desired outcomes with clarity and conviction. Then watch as the universe aligns with your dreams.

— **Sylvester McNutt III,** *Live the Life You Deserve*

Visualize the reality you wish to create with passion and deep emotion. See yourself in the moments of triumph, feel the sensations of success, and let your visions guide you toward manifestation.

— **Sylvester McNutt III,** *Live the Life You Deserve*

Break free from the chains of a soulless job and embrace a mindset of positivity and hope. Shift your focus to growth, set healthy boundaries, and open yourself to new opportunities. Your job is a choice. Choose jobs that align with you, with the lifestyle you want to live.

— **Sylvester McNutt III,** *Live the Life You Deserve*

Break free from the chains of who you were and of obsessive thinking about your past. Overthinking and grading everything will never make us happy. Give yourself permission to allow thoughts to pass naturally. Learn to allow thoughts to come and go, especially those that do not serve you. Begin to intentionally create thoughts that speak on your power, on your possibilities, on how beautiful life is. Begin to see your thoughts as sacred and important. Begin to see your thoughts as a vessel for creation of the life you are worthy of living. Use your tongue to speak about your life in a hopeful and positive way—there's immense power in thoughts and in words, and it's your duty to use them to your advantage.

— **Sylvester McNutt III,** *Live the Life You Deserve*

Delve into the depths of your consciousness, tap into your innermost desires, and empower yourself to take bold action. Embrace the law of deliberate creation and step into the life you deserve. Being bold and brave is the only way to create what you deserve. Most people are afraid of failure and what others may say. You cannot concern yourself with such banal viewpoints. Your success will make your soul feel engaged and important, and you deserve that.

— **Sylvester McNutt III,** *Live the Life You Deserve*

Commit to your dreams with unwavering dedication and relentless effort. See yourself actualizing what is playing out in your head. Rise early, live passionately, and let your actions carve out the outcomes you want to feel most. Harness the power of deliberate creation by consciously controlling your thoughts. Your thoughts shape your actions, and your actions shape your experiences. Choose thoughts that align with your desires. Your journey begins the day that you overcommit to your dreams.

— **Sylvester McNutt III,** *Live the Life You Deserve*

## HOW TO CREATE YOUR DREAM LIFE— FROM ONE DREAMER TO ANOTHER

I went for all my dreams in life when I was a kid, as a teenager, and now as an adult. I achieved some of them exactly how I imagined. Others manifested differently but gave me experiences I didn't even know I needed. Now, as a parent, I am tasked with empowering my kids to follow their dreams. My message to them is the same message I give you:

Never give up. Never listen to people who are afraid and do not have the vision that you have been given. It does not matter if you do not have all the data to align your dreams; you don't need it. You'll find your path along the way. If these dreams keep calling, it's time to answer. You will make mistakes, and that's okay. Just bounce back and be mindful of the language you use. Speak love, power, and life into yourself every day. I love you and know you can do it.

I have a career that I love. I checked that box around age 25 and have been able to keep it ever since. A lot of people never go for what they want; therefore, it's literally impossible for them to have it. I am fortunate and humbled to know that I still have great health. While I feel blessed, it would be disingenuous not to honor the sacrifices, hard work, and dedication that went into the journey. I have a powerful community that fulfills me in every way: family, friends, sports friends, party friends, travel friends, a passionate lover, kids who want to play all the time, coworkers who are healthy and want to get the job done, a men's group, and so on. As I prepare myself mentally to enter elderhood, I must acknowledge that this "dream life" was created intentionally. My mission is to peel the curtain back so you can gain context on the ingredients that went into the vessel that cooked this recipe.

To me, writing is one of my hobbies and always has been; it's something that I am going to do no matter what happens externally. Yes, I've sold millions of books, and I'm signed with Hay House, the most prestigious publisher of personal development work in the world. I'm one of the most-read authors in the world. I've done hundreds of interviews and have written at least 50,000 pieces of content across the Internet. I could go on and on about how the external world may perceive my work today.

I have a successful coaching practice that has assisted thousands of people in their missions to live the life they deserve. I'm writing to you from my favorite coffee shop in Colombia a few weeks before my birthday. I can buy anything I want even though I don't require much. For my birthday, I am going to run a six-mile race in Sonoma, California, and drink fine wine and dine with a few of my good friends. I have another book idea that I am going to pitch after I turn this one in, and I know Hay House is going to love the idea. I'm not going to take a day off when I turn this book in—nope, I am literally going to start working on the next book proposal and spend a lot more time having fun, getting in the gym, and living life with my community. I am going to go deeper in my coaching practice and double down on as much learning as possible. I need to stay committed to the work that has created and sustained this "dream life"—but don't interpret that as I am not going to rest, heal, and recover because I do that every day.

Now, when you hear this, it can evoke a lot of different responses, none of which I am responsible for. But please, think about the conscious thoughts that you had—those thoughts are literally going to power your plight to live the life you deserve. Did you think, *Yes, reading that he is living his dream life inspires me to know that I can too,* or was the subconscious thought more like, *I'm stuck; I'll never be able to live my dream life?* Think about that. As creators of our experience, we must always be aware of these subconscious thoughts and reactions that pop up. When you hear or see someone doing well, simply say, "Good for them; they deserve it." This type of energy and mindset is abundance, and it is not laced with envy, jealousy, or lack.

My responsibility is to tell you how I was able to live the life I deserve and how I was able to create my dream job. It wasn't about my education, some immaculate plan or strategy, or an elite level of intelligence. Nope, the only factors that were used—factors that we all have access to—are extreme self-belief, unwillingness to settle for failure, and a commitment to the art of deliberate creation.

I choose exactly what I want, and I say no to anything that keeps me out of what I want. I am willing to suffer if that suffering is going to deliver me what I want—but my suffering has clear and defined boundaries.

I am willing to force my dreams. I'm willing to fight for my dreams. I'm willing to be embarrassed for my dreams. I understand that these emotional states are temporary and that I am strong enough to withstand them. I am willing to look like a fool, to lose, to be without nothing. I am willing to have people call me names and leave me stranded. I am willing to lose everything I have at one point in time as I know the subtraction of *what was* is the only way to create *what will be.*

I live my dream life because I didn't compare what I wanted to anyone else. I am authentic with my desires;

I am extremely specific with what I want and how I am going to go about it.

Now, am I telling you I have a perfect life with no stress or issues? No, come on now. I have problems. Stressors. Issues. Complaints. Things I wish I could change about the world and even within. But I was able to build my dream life because I was clear on my value system.

## SHARPEN YOUR VALUE SYSTEM TO CREATE THE LIFE YOU WANT

As you design the life you deserve, you need to get clear on your value system. Once you draw a line in the sand, you get clear on how you are going to move and what your life is going to be like. You become a magnet for what you want, for what you crave, and you live in alignment with it. Most people take whatever was given to them and never get clear on their values. Get clear on the things that you will and will not entertain.

In your notebook or through an imagination exercise, I want you to consider your value system. I'm going to include these same 11 questions as journaling prompts at the end of this chapter, but I'm also going to give you my own answers for them here. The purpose of these questions is to get you aligned with the values that value the lived outcome you want.

I promise you my next meal that if you sit with these specific questions and be mindful of how you craft your answers, you will get more than 50 percent ahead on the mission of creating the life you deserve. These questions will also be the building blocks for how you can be a deliberate creator as you build and sustain your rituals of play, abundance, and joy.

It's special for me to share these questions with you as I answered them myself shortly before I went full-time into being an author. While I don't have that notebook anymore, I do know what my answers are in the present, and they parallel the ones I came up with way back when I did this exercise myself. It's possible that you can benefit from hearing my answers for my journey, but please don't let them be the baseline for you. We are different people, and if you do this exercise from an authentic space, I promise you will find the light you are looking for.

**What is your perspective on time?**

I believe that I don't know what time is or how to explain it, but I know I want to use most of time to have freedom to choose to do what I want, where I want, and how I want.

**How do you view work?**

I believe having a career that gives you purpose is essential. I don't believe it needs to fulfill every aspect of your life; in fact, that seems unrealistic. I find most jobs to be useless, mundane, and boring. Therefore, I want to do a job like writing, because for my brain, it's hard and engaging and forces me to use one of my powers, which is understanding language. It's a job that I also feel adds value to the world. One of my main gripes working at Verizon is that I was selling a product that I knew was going to do harm, which was smartphones. I got out to sell something that was more aligned with my soul.

LIVE THE LIFE YOU DESERVE

## How do you view play?

I view play the same way I view work: as something that is essential. I need work and play, and I see them as the same thing. Some of the things that I play at I could never earn income with. For example, I love basketball, but I'm five nine, so there was simply no way I was about to be on a roster averaging 15 points a game. But I found daily walks, yoga, writing, meditation, cooking, dancing, arts, and so many other ways to play. Now that I am a father, I play with my kids. Play is necessary, and I believe in building a life around it equal to or greater than the way we build vocation.

## Are you willing to suffer?

Yes, I am. I will suffer and sacrifice if I know there's value in it. I don't want to suffer just because it sounds good. I want my suffering to be aligned with the life I deserve. I would walk 10 miles to fish if I needed to get the freshest salmon in the river. I will be outside for hours in the garden if that is going to give us fresh veggies and fruits. I will write 1,000 words every day for 10 years if in my heart I know that will sharpen my skill and allow me to write a great book. I will do all the training necessary to get in the best shape of my life, even if it feels like a bag of pain to me. And maybe suffering is only halfway correct here. Maybe we should also note that a commitment to the process may not always be pretty, ideal, or perfect. Yes, I love being an author, but I hate that other people judge your work. I love traveling, but I don't like most of the people at the airport who are stressed. Suffering is necessary—with boundaries.

**Are you willing to say yes to what you want?**

Yes, living the life you deserve is about saying yes to what you want. This is elementary and mandatory.

**Are you willing to say no to distractions?**

One hundred percent. . . . Get out of my way!

**Are you fully focused on what you want to create or just sort of focused?**

The word *focus* is interesting. I want to highlight that we all have a different amount of focus and differences in how long we can stay focused. Comparison is not the answer. Focus here is simply about the frequency with which you touch something. Writing daily is the best way to find rhythm in your writing, but writing three to four times a week also yields results. Writing for two hours every Saturday could also get you to where you need to be. Frequency varies based on the individual. I feel focused, and when I don't have focus, I don't force it. I think obsessions are fine, but we have to be authentic. You may not have the energy needed to focus, and forcing an obsession works for some but not everyone. I preach duality and authenticity above everything else. So for me, yes, I'm fully focused and ready to roll.

**Are you going to settle for what you want, something close to it, or anything?**

I like this question because there is nuance and practicality in the answer. I don't want to be dogmatic in my ways with anything. Sometimes, I will settle for what makes the most sense at that moment. I am forever in the flow of life, and I trust that everything will work out for me. Most of the time, I will get exactly what I want, as I know how powerful I am as a creator. And the other times will be when I will get close to what I want, but there will be some sacrifice or it won't be perfect, and I am okay with that. I think people use spiritual language to make it seem like the only option for happiness and wellness is getting *exactly* what you want, and that's not playful enough for me. If the outcome has elements of what I want, plus it surprises me and brings me pieces I never expected, I would never be mad.

### What is your attitude like?

I have a good attitude about what I am capable of, but my weakness is not trusting other people as much as I could. I would benefit from learning how to trust others more. Not everyone, but those who have good energy and have a track record of being responsible.

### Are you going to be a victor or a victim?

I am a victor. I am not a victim. Simple.

### Are you doing the great work that is aligned with the outcome you seek?

I am willing to do what it takes to create the life I want.

# JOURNAL PROMPTS: YOUR VALUE SYSTEM

- What is your perspective on time?

- How do you view work?

- How do you view play?

- Are you willing to suffer?

- Are you willing to say yes to what you want?

- Are you willing to say no to distractions?

- Are you fully focused on what you want to create or just sort of focused?

- Are you going to settle for what you want, something close to it, or anything?

- What is your attitude like?

- Are you going to be a victor or a victim?

- Are you doing the great work that is aligned with the outcome you seek?

One of the best parts of life is when you recognize that, yes, there is a lot you cannot control, and there is a lot that you can—it's a duality. When people speak about feeling empowered, it's because they know that there is a lot they can control, and they focus there. They make a home there. You can design your life. Every day you have air in your lungs, you can design the life you want. Fall in love with this process because the more you love it, the easier it is.

— **Sylvester McNutt III,** *Live the Life You Deserve*

I need you to understand that you have the power to design your life. I am teaching my son every single day that he has more power than he realizes. If I could go back and talk to myself when I was talking like a victim, when I was speaking in a limited way, I would tell him to stop instantly. If I could sit in your brain for 10 minutes, you would hear me say over and over, "You can do this. You can design your life. You are powerful beyond measure. Your aura is growing. Your energy is getting big enough for this. Step up and step in." Ninety percent of the game of life is energy, 5 percent is knowledge, and the other 5 percent is letting go. Get your energy right!

— **Sylvester McNutt III,** *Live the Life You Deserve*

Give yourself permission to design the life you want. Most people don't need more. They just need to be better with their leadership abilities and discipline. Everything you want and need is on the other side of your discipline and your ability to lead yourself and those around you. Step up and step into shoes that have the widest footprint. Take up space and go after everything you deserve.

— **Sylvester McNutt III,** *Live the Life You Deserve*

CHAPTER 7

# MAKING SPACE FOR THE GREAT WORK OF GRIEVING AND LETTING GO

The only way to move ahead on a monkey bar is to release the grip of the hand behind you as you swing forward. To get the momentum and energy you want to progress, you have to release what was and, sometimes, what is. Letting go is the path to freedom—the path to living the life you deserve. The human experience has hundreds of moments in which we need to grieve, heal, and make peace with what is and what was.

Human beings have many basic motivations. One of them is to find meaning and purpose. How can we find meaning and purpose if we are holding on to stories, ideas, emotions, and habits that keep us distracted from our purpose and meaning? It's time to let go.

— **Sylvester McNutt III,** *Live the Life You Deserve*

Letting go, grieving, and acknowledging these vessels and voids are truly about the descent; they are vital alchemical processes on our way to our humanity. It's about going down in the psyche and exploring the depths of the soul—going down into your heart and journey with compassion and honor. This part of the journey is about reconnecting with your roots and developing a connection to the soil, to the soil of your life. This is the part of your journey where we begin to find reverence and honor for our stories, for our roots, and we begin to water and nourish them.

— **Sylvester McNutt III,** *Live the Life You Deserve*

As you pursue the life you deserve, you also release what is no longer in alignment. There will be hard work and sacrifice, and there will be grief. I want to validate the sadness that can come with change. *Letting go* is a phrase that we use all the time, but each psyche registers it differently. Perhaps letting go of pieces of who we were feels like a death, an ego-death, a death of identity. Perhaps inner changes will also cause external changes to our friendships and relationships. Changing yourself in any way has a ripple effect and may change outer relationships, which may cause a great deal of excitement and joy but also cause pain and confusion. I want you to know that at least one person gets you. As you fall deeper in love with creating the life you deserve, you are never alone in the pain of releasing a friend, habit, or piece of your own identity to make this necessary change.

I want to be clear: when I am referring to "letting go" in this chapter and book, I'm talking about letting go of past identities, past emotions, and stories. The lens here is purely intrinsic, and the purpose behind it is to shift your energy, focus, and time to purpose and meaning through mastery and using the law of attraction.

As you begin to "let go," you must also understand that there is a duality: as you let go and release, there is still something you will hold on to. If you let go of a drinking habit, you may also release the friends you have known for the last five years. This is a lot to hold as you gain your health, your freedom, more money, and better health. But then, there could be a void of loneliness and pain as you don't connect with who you've known, whether it's your drinking buddies or even yourself, as you learn who you are without that aspect.

Human beings have many basic motivations. One of them is to find meaning and purpose. How can we find meaning and purpose if we are holding on to stories, ideas, emotions, and habits that keep us distracted from our purpose and meaning? It's time to let go.

## UNDERSTANDING THE NATURE OF GRIEF

I wonder if the root of unhappiness for many is the pursuit of happiness itself. Yes, happiness is a powerful state of being, but it's not the only one. Being a happy human should not be the goal. Happiness comes and goes. Lean in and savor happiness when it comes, but give yourself permission to feel anger, grief, and other pains that are human.

Living the life you deserve means being real. Sometimes you will be happy and sometimes you won't. A healthy mind and body acknowledge the authentic emotions that arise, and they learn how to process, cope, and manage what is. Give yourself permission to be real.

I believe that our Western world does a terrible job at talking about death, grieving, the loss of friendships and family, and the loss of self. I feel as if it is my duty to include this chapter in the book so we can have more language and space and the invitation to visit the depths of grief, letting go, and moving on.

Lean in to the duality that when you grow, mature, and align with the life you want to live, it's possible that you will have grief—and you are capable of holding both. No matter how much money you make, no matter how much success you achieve, and no matter how highly you think about yourself, you will need to grieve in life.

A Swiss-American psychiatrist, Elisabeth Kübler-Ross, first introduced her five stages grief model in her book, *On Death and Dying*. The book was based on her work with terminally ill patients. Some people see this model as a linear process, but if you've lost someone or something or a piece of yourself, you know that it may not be. In my experience, as someone who has been to over 10 funerals and lost lots of people, this process is not linear. If you are grieving, give yourself the grace to understand that your process is unique to you. Give yourself permission to honor your unique self and where you are in life.

Kübler-Ross described these five stages of grief as:[1]

1. Denial

2. Anger

3. Bargaining

4. Depression

5. Acceptance

Grief is universal. If you investigate this world, you'd see so much division in ideologies, in political parties, and in countries, but something that is universal to human experience is grief. We all experience loss. I would invite you to understand that your mortal enemy has grief and so does your lover—it is deeply human, and our grieving processes need to be acknowledged and held with love. I would argue that this model is extremely simplistic, and I don't say *simplistic* as a negative. I say *simplistic* for most Westerners because we think we should follow a certain path for everything. Grief is something that transcends the thinking brain; it is an emotional state with depth. You may flow through and jump stages in your grief process; honor your unique self as you do.

I experienced a death where I felt immediately at acceptance, which was truly dissociation or ignoring the feelings. Then four months later, I felt denial and anger, which confused me. I remember thinking, *I thought I was over this.* But then I watched a video by triple board-certified neuropsychologist Dr. Judy Ho in which she affirmed there is no wrong way to grieve. Ho also said that everyone has to have their own boundaries around grief.[2] This means that we're all entitled to do whatever we need to do to get through our day, to choose how and when we grieve. To hear that from someone who is an expert on the subject felt like permission, like an invitation to create a vessel for grieving. Just remember, grief is not a linear process.

Since we are talking about the inner lens of change, you may feel grief as you attempt to let go of a bad habit or your old self. I remember when I committed to not drinking for a full year—I felt grief. Even though I was excited to be taking control of my health, my brain, and my bank account and living an empowered life, I still felt a deep grief about it. I felt like there were some people I simply couldn't hang out with because they wouldn't be able to accept that I didn't want to drink anymore.

Nowadays, I still don't drink very much because of that year-long experiment. I enjoy wine and will keep a few bottles at the house, but nothing like it was before. I used to do social drinking with friends two nights per week, but my body told me that was too much. Now, I'll go months without drinking; then, if I feel called to, I will do so without any guilt or shame. I try to live freely without labels, and that works for me. I invite you to honor your unique self and honor what works for you. My goal is to be authentic with where I am, to be self-aware, and to be intuitively connected to my mind and body.

## THE FIVE GATES OF GRIEF

My personal invitation to you as you enter and engage in grief is that you simply do that—engage it. I believe some of us are being taught to just get over it and move on, and I don't feel as if that's required. Francis Weller, who is one of my favorite authors and teachers, says, "Don't think that you need to muscle your way through your sorrow, you can't. Grief is waiting for the village to show up, your grief should never be private. Your village can be small. We mainly need someone to listen deeply to our sorrow. We need people to listen our sorrow and tells us that it matters."[3]

I found Francis Weller's work when I needed it most, in 2020. Yes, in part because of the pandemic we faced, but more because I had become a new parent—the loss of being "Sylvester with no kids," which is all I knew for my entire life. I was mentally prepared to embody the role of father, to be a protector, leader, friend, and provider. I was not prepared to *grieve* the loss of who I was prior to then. I didn't even know I was grieving when I was; so many of us are living like that. Sad some days, and we don't know why. Upset some days, and nothing triggered it. If this sounds familiar, it's possible that you are grieving.

In his book, *The Wild Edge of Sorrow*, Francis Weller explores the five gates of grief, using it as a metaphor to show the many ways that loss touches our hearts and souls in this life. I want to share them with you here as they gave me more language and space when I was trying to understand my own grief, and I hope they do the same for you. He offers them as the ability to understand the depth of loss as a human on a poetic, soulful, and more divine level.[4]

- **Everything We Love, We Will Lose:** This gate acknowledges the truth of impermanence. It is the grief experienced with the loss of someone or something you love, including your family and friends. It is also the experience of illness and the resulting loss of vitality, one's previous life, even one's work and relationships.

- **The Places That Have Not Known Love:** The second gate is through shame and the rejection of any part of yourself as defective or unlovable. Self-hatred and contempt cause you to be disconnected from your soul and to reject healing and community. Self-compassion is needed for your regrets, trauma, and childhood wounds.

- **The Sorrows of the World:** Communal grief, recognizing the pain and losses of the world around you, is the third gate. This is the experience of the soul of the world, the field of consciousness within nature. It is the feeling of emptiness and loss of connection with the living earth.

- **What We Expected and Did Not Receive:** The fourth gate is a profound sense of lack due to being born into a society that failed to give us what we were designed to expect: love, community, intimacy, a relationship with the earth, a connection to the sacred. It manifests as a vague sadness, emptiness, and longing that is difficult to name. You have a diminished sense of who you truly are.

- **Ancestral Grief:** This is the unacknowledged and untended sorrow carried within your body and psyche of those who came before you. It is also the loss of connection to the land, language, imagination, rituals, songs, and stories of your ancestors, especially because of modern society's focus on "progress."

When I use my mantra that is also this book title, *live the life you deserve*, I use it as an invitation to our greatest and highest self. That invitation doesn't always mean love and light, or positive vibes, or that everything is about ascension and getting better. Letting go, grieving, and acknowledging these vessels and voids are truly about the descent; they are vital alchemical processes on our way to our humanity. It's about going down in the psyche and exploring the depths of the soul—going down into your heart and journey with compassion and honor. This part of the journey is about reconnecting with your roots and developing a connection to the soil of your life. This is the part of your journey where we begin to find reverence and honor for our stories, for our roots, and we begin to water and nourish them.

When I lost my preparenthood identity, I felt a deep ancestral grief as I felt the pressure of generations of African American parents upon my broad shoulders. I felt the legacy of what my parents and grandparents and their grandparents created, and I felt a call to step up, to step through, to step in. This stepping up, which was purely internal, made me feel like I had to do more, be more, and create and achieve more. This pressure helped and hurt as it made me grow up, but it was heavier than the Golden Gate Bridge.

I also felt a deep pain when my son was born in 2020 as travel was shut down because of the pandemic. Therefore, my mother and entire family back in Chicago were unable to be present with us in Phoenix, Arizona. I was sad, angry, and disappointed as I always imagined being circled by family at least a little bit during the sacred threshold of bringing a life into the world—but there would be none of that. Francis Weller talks about that as the second and fourth gates of grief.

I felt a deep grief when I became a father because I also did not have my father on this earth anymore. I couldn't call him and ask advice or hear stories about his experience. He transitioned to the death realm about nine years prior to my son being born. Again, grief is deeply personal, and I wish my father were able to see this version of me. I was able to chase my dreams, fail, and keep pushing past my failures, as he always taught me. I was able to make something meaningful out of my life. Ultimately, as parents, that is all we want for our children—for them to find meaning, for them to grow into their highest self. I wish I could've shown him this version of me so he would've known that the work worked and that his efforts mattered.

As I sat in a great deal of joy and excitement for my son when he was born, I was also met with a deep curtain of this ancestral grief. I was able to live out dreams for all of us, and still, I felt bad about them not being able to witness my results, which is a direct extension of their leaderships, their examples, and most importantly their sacrifices that I'll never be able to fully understand.

I have never once in my life ever heard another parent mention the grief they feel once their son or daughter was born, yet I know that I am not alone in these feelings. Now, at least one person has spoken on it, so we have permission to bring this conversation to our society.

If you too felt a grief when your kids were born, I want you to know that you are not alone. And in the future, when you have kids, if you do, if you experience grief and feel confused by it, please remember that you are not alone and that your grief is valid, normal, and justified.

## "GRIEFALLS" AND NON-DEATH LOSS

You might be sad due to a non-death loss—a loss in which your life changes but everything and everyone is still alive. No matter how silly or miniscule to others it seems, you 100 percent have permission to grieve the losses that are dear to you.

I just finished reading a great book, *Moving on Doesn't Mean Letting Go*, by licensed clinical social worker Gina Moffa. In her book, she goes into detail about the *griefall,* what she calls the free fall after major loss. She describes it: "As my own griefall continued to unravel before me, there were no sparkles or inspiring quotes. Instead, it felt like I had tripped on the sidewalk and fallen headfirst down a bottomless void."[5] I am loving the imagery of see-ing grief as a void, as a space that is vast and wide, deep and bold. We began to examine and observe the *prima materia* (prime matter) of our life, as alchemists, as cre-ators. It's incumbent upon us to travel into these voids when life asks us to.

Gina goes on to mention in her testimony that when she was grieving, she needed friends, family, and con-nection, so she ventured down to her local restaurant in New York City, a place where everybody knew her name. That night, when her intention was to seek community, happened to also be the very night that the bartender looked at her and said, "I'm sorry, Gina, we are closing our business tonight." So now she was grieving both the loss of her mother and the loss of the restaurant. Gina calls this a *non-death loss*: "They don't seem like they should matter as much because, well, *no one died.* At the core of all loss, though, is attachment. We form emotional connections to the people, places, pets, and things in our lives in ways that don't always make sense for other people."[6]

Reading those lines felt like a breath of fresh air. They helped me understand that my grief is unique and normal, valid, and okay. I hope that, no matter what you may name as your grief or what components you could mention in your grieving process, you know that it is valid and justified and that you are not alone. Even if it is a non-death loss, you are still allowed to grieve, to heal, and to honor what was.

## JOURNAL PROMPTS: GRIEF AND CHANGE

- What might you need to let go of and release in order to live the life you deserve? Consider whether the fear and grief of losing your current identity might be one of the things holding you back from living as your highest self.

- Write about a time when you experienced a big change in your life. Do you see any of your feelings captured within the five gates of grief?

- Write about how a fear of change is stopping you from going to the next level. What are you afraid of? What would happen if you stepped into this fear and took the risks or made the changes?

- Sometimes we are dealing with an immense amount of grief, and we somehow expect success, thriving, and forward movement. Is it possible that what you need right now is stillness and to simply be without the pressure of doing? Write about where you are on the journey of doing versus being.

When we talk about creating the life we want, it's always seen as a positive thing, which it is, but it can also come with negative consequences. I need you to understand that setting boundaries, having discipline, and getting serious about your life can require sacrifice but also will bring you a great deal of joy and focus. Your brain wants something to focus on. Your soul needs something to inspire you. You were not sent here to do a million things at once. Use the next year of your life to make one dream come true or set one goal and to stay locked in as you work toward it.

— **Sylvester McNutt III,** *Live the Life You Deserve*

Give yourself permission to grieve. Life is not just about success, working hard, and creating opportunity. Honor the dead. Honor the pieces of you that have passed. Allow yourself to feel that random grief and sorrow that will come up from time to time. Allow yourself to feel the depths of the human experience, for it gives you access to healing, to authenticity, to your highest self.

— **Sylvester McNutt III,** *Live the Life You Deserve*

Your grief matters. You deserve to share it with someone or with a small community of people who have the space to hold you and see you. Grief is not something that only you feel—we all do. Give yourself permission to share your grief in the right space with people who care.

— **Sylvester McNutt III**, *Live the Life You Deserve*

If you are used to being strong and figuring things out, please give yourself permission to use a community, to use friends and family. The strong friend often carries burdens that they do not have to carry. If you are the strong friend, understand these words: it's okay to grieve, it's okay to not know, and it's okay to be tired and need help.

— **Sylvester McNutt III**, *Live the Life You Deserve*

For the "Strong Friend":

You might have become this way because of trauma, because of what your parents lacked, or because of what was required to survive. Congratulations—you figured it out by being strong. But we know that on the inside, you too need love, you too need to be nurtured, and you too need to be cared for. There are people who want to have your back, and all I ask of you is that you let them. There are good people who want to be in your corner and who have the skills to support you— let them. As strong people, we assume we must always be strong all the time. Remember, strength is also about authenticity; some days you just won't have the strength to lend. Heal. Recharge. Let your community love you and continue to thrive. Your community loves how strong you are; just know you are allowed compassion and space as well.

— **Sylvester McNutt III,** *Live the Life You Deserve*

## CHAPTER 8

# GIVE YOURSELF PERMISSION TO FEEL JOY

Accept the invitation to enjoy life for what it is, for what it isn't, and for all that it may be. Open yourself up to joy and laughter, to play and fun, and to all the richness in life. Give yourself permission to feel joy.

The law of attraction is a powerful tool that we can use to deliberately create and design the life we deserve. Keep your heart open to the idea that you are worthy of joy and that joy is common, it comes frequently, you attract it, and you create it.

— **Sylvester McNutt III,** *Live the Life You Deserve*

I have been in deep spaces of grief, anger, mental unruliness—we all have at one point or another because we are human. That level of pain or suffering is not just you or me. It's human. Over time, I've learned to practice joy when I am happy and feel like I'm on the top of the world, and I practice joy when things are not going well, when life is beating me down, and when I need a break. The point to remember is that joy is always accessible.

— **Sylvester McNutt III,** *Live the Life You Deserve*

*Be the kind of person who welcomes joy.*

*Be the kind of person who welcomes joy.*

*Be the kind of person who welcomes joy.*

*Be the kind of person who welcomes joy.*

*Be the kind of person who welcomes joy.*

*Be the kind of person who welcomes joy.*

*Be the kind of person who welcomes joy.*

*Be the kind of person who welcomes joy.*

*Be the kind of person who welcomes joy.*

*Be the kind of person who welcomes joy.*

*Be the kind of person who welcomes joy.*

*Be the kind of person who welcomes joy.*

*Be the kind of person who welcomes joy.*

*Be the kind of person who welcomes joy.*

*Be the kind of person who welcomes joy.*

The law of attraction is a powerful tool that we can use to deliberately create and design the life we deserve. Keep your heart open to the idea that you are worthy of joy and that joy is common, it comes frequently, you attract it, and you create it.

When I interviewed neuropsychologist Dr. Jen Wolkin, she said, "Our minds are more powerful than we realize. We can think our way into positive thoughts and a positive frame of mind. From that place of positivity, we can create more healing, more compassion, and more joy."[1] Graduate from the idea that joy and happiness is an emotion that comes. Instead, believe in the deliberate power of creation—believe that you can create a magnetic force field to *attract* this energy.

## ONE SIMPLE ROUTINE TO CREATE JOY

We all have a morning routine, whether we call it that or not. There are a set of habits you do every morning to start your day—so why not make them habits and ideas that pour a powerful emotion into you and the people you love? Let's call it the "joy routine." The purpose of this routine is to create joy, to be a magnet for it, to be a deliberate creator of this energy.

The one simple habit that you should integrate starting tomorrow is this: smile at yourself in the mirror and say aloud that you are welcoming of joy and love. If you want to rewire your brain and genuinely change your life, start tomorrow with this practice. Do it after you do your hygiene routine and get dressed, before you go start your work or school day. Stop every single day and smile. Check your outfit and make sure it's up to par. Make sure your face, mouth, and hair are clean. Look at yourself with respect and reverence, and say these affirmations aloud:

*I attract joy.*

*I create joy.*

*I love myself.*

*I create love.*

*People love me because I create joy.*

*People love me because I share joy.*

*People love me because I give them permission to feel joy.*

*I love me because I give myself permission to feel joy.*

And then do it again tomorrow and again the following day. It takes 5 to 15 seconds, and you will feel the benefits. If this practice does not work, I will personally come sweep your kitchen, clean the counters, and make you a meal. But I promise I won't have to because you will *feel* the amount of joy shift.

What this practice does is sharpen and attune you to the emotions of joy. Think about it like this: if I go to your kitchen and try to cut fish or bread with a dull knife, I could get hurt with the dull blade and the stress will make me mad. But if I bring my knife-sharpening kit and sharpen your knives so they are better than brand-new, then what? Sharpening yourself emotionally to be in alignment with joy makes you better able to feel it and identify it.

Speaking of food, do you pray? Do you say a blessing or express gratitude for the meal, for the nourishment that you are about to receive? I notice that many people nowadays devour their food—why do we do this? Cherish the food. Put love and good energy into the food. Shift your mindset to make food communal if possible; if you are eating solo, take time to bring joy to your plate before you eat.

I smile at every meal before I eat it. I'm not going to stop either. People who have eaten with me are now going to watch me to see if I am lying; I'm not. At every meal I intentionally stop, create a moment of joy, and then eat. The reason I do this is to stay in energetic alignment with joy. I like this as a "backup joy routine" because as a parent, sometimes when I wake up, I don't have all my time to myself. Sometimes, I can't do my joy practice in the morning, so before my meal is an opportunity to go ahead and cultivate that joy.

You might be thinking, why is he talking about joy so much? The American Psychological Association (APA) defines joy as a "feeling of extreme gladness, delight, or exaltation of the spirit arising from a sense of well-being or satisfaction."[2] Joy is not the same emotion in the body as happiness, however. We use *joy* and *happiness* in an interchangeable way in our society, but it's important we understand their differences.

*Happiness* is how we feel about our lives over a duration of time and has to do with things that help us see if we have a sense of meaning and purpose. Are we connected to friends and family? Are we connected to our work? Is there something bigger than us that we are fighting for? Those elements play into our perspective of happiness.

*Joy* is an immediate experience that is often observable and measurable through physical expression, like two arms up in excitement, smiling and laughing, and moving your body almost in an uncontrollable way triggered by something positive. Joy activates the parasympathetic nervous system, which promotes feelings of peace and calm. It is associated with increased energy, confidence, and self-esteem. You can find joy daily, even when your happiness is not there. A person enduring a depressive month or so due to job loss or a breakup would tell you that they are not happy. But it's important to remember in these unhappy places we still have the opportunity to access and activate joy. That person who is in the breakup phase could still experience joy when they go to a comedy show with their best friend *and* they can still be unhappy overall.

*Happiness is perspective over time; joy is
more direct and in the moment.*

Can you see how getting dressed first and then doing a
joy practice is going to inspire you to feel like your highest
self? I have been depressed. I have been sad. I have been in
deep spaces of grief, anger, and mental unruliness—we all
have at one point or another because we are human. That
level of pain or suffering is not just you or me. It's human.
Over time, I've learned to practice joy when I am happy and
feel like I'm on top of the world, and I practice joy when
things are not going well, when life is beating me down, or
when I need a break. The point to remember is that joy is
always accessible.

Now, one might ask, is it toxic positivity to attempt to
access joy when you are not happy? My simple response to
that is no. In life, we have a lot of emotions that are reactions, and others that we can create. I accept that I have
the power to sharpen and attune my life to joy and happiness. Do you? If you accept that as well, then that means
you know that happiness is not possible every single day,
no matter what happens, and you can hold that through
most situations we still have the ability to access joy. Two
things can be true.

## BECOME A HOME FOR JOY

When you become a "home for joy," you enhance your
relationships with others. This subtle communication hack
can change any relationship, new or old. It begins with
the ability to think outside of yourself to recognize when
your friend, family member, or partner is making a bid.
In psychology, a bid is an attempt to connect, and it can
take various forms. It might be a simple question, a shared

observation, or even a gesture. When you become attuned to these bids for connection and respond with genuine interest and enthusiasm, you create a positive feedback loop in your relationships.[3]

Sometimes we dismiss bids because we aren't interested in the subject. For example, your husband may love his fantasy football chat, his team, and the thrill of watching games to see if he wins that week. You may think fantasy football is a waste of time, money, and energy. Remember, two things can be true! Living the life you deserve in this context would mean investing energy into the relationship to grow joy. Instead of acting uninterested or even telling him that it is a waste of time, become interested. Ask him questions about it. Ask him how he feels about the team at the top of the week. This creates the space for him to share the entire story and experience with you as he goes through it. It's these subtle things in life that when we create space and be a home for others, it gives them power to stand in their unique self. The more you allow others around you to be their unique self, the more permission you have to do the same.

By acknowledging and reciprocating these attempts to connect, you foster a sense of emotional intimacy and trust. Joy begins to flow naturally in these moments of connection, and your relationships become even more fulfilling. As you continue to practice this approach, you'll find that joy not only resides within you but also radiates from you, enriching both your life and the lives of those around you.

## OPEN YOUR LIFE TO MORE JOY BY TAKING TIME TO PLAY

As the sun gently filtered through the curtains, I woke up to my energetic four-year-old son bouncing on the edge of my bed like Spider-Man, webbing imaginary bad guys. "Daddy, it's time to go to daycare," he exclaimed with excitement. I smiled at him, but deep down I felt a pang of guilt. I had been working tirelessly on two books at once, plus I'd started travelling again, both for work and personal reasons. As we got ready to leave, my son looked up at me with those innocent eyes and said, "Don't go to work today, Daddy. You work too much—just play with me."

His words struck a chord in my heart.

"I have to go to work, son," I say. It's an automatic response. I have been conditioned to prioritize providing, earning, and making things to drive profit to my business.

I considered his offer as I fastened him into his car seat. I knew he needed more quality time with me, and maybe, just maybe, I needed it too. For some reason, I sat on the seesaw of decision making as I drove him toward daycare. As I began to listen to that voice that was screaming inside me, I felt a moment of clarity and made a bold decision.

I listened to my son's plea and called off work for the day. Granted, I work for myself, so I have the freedom to do that. But I'll be honest with you: most entrepreneurs work every day or as often as possible. Especially when you love what you do, it's easy to be inside the business every single day—there is always something to be done, a call to make, a client to support, a book to write, a retreat to plan. Work never runs out.

Today, it felt different. As we pulled up to the street where his daycare was, instead of turning right, I kept going straight. I pulled up to the park that was right down the street. I felt him looking around with his naturally curious demeanor.

In excitement, my son said, "Daddy, this is not the daycare. Where are we?"

"Today, son, we are going to play and let the universe guide us to where we need to be," I said.

He screamed, "Yes, we are going to play. We are going to play! We are going to *play!*"

We hit the slides, ran after one another, and climbed the jungle gym. I watched him run around, laughing and exploring, and I couldn't help but join in on his infectious joy. We played tag and had a playful race across the grass. The world seemed to slow down as I embraced the simplicity of play.

Next, we went to the children's museum. We'd taken him when he was younger, but it was under the pandemic rules of 2020 and 2021, and he'd only been around a year old or younger, so he didn't really enjoy it. Or should I say *I* didn't enjoy it because taking a baby anywhere at that young of an age was more of a job versus a fun activity. Together, we roamed through the exhibits, learning about dinosaurs, space, and history. There were obstacles to run through and climb—we did it all. I saw the engagement in his eyes, and I realized that play is about not only having fun but also discovering and experiencing new things.

For lunchtime, we found a random brunch spot and ordered eggs, fruit, café con leche, and some soup. We laughed, shared stories, and enjoyed the delicious food. He threw a fit when some of his food fell off his fork, and I gave him the support he needed during his meltdown. And that was that—he got over it, and the party kept going. We went to the mall. I bought us matching shoes and treated us to a fresh smoothie with fruits and veggies.

That day taught me some valuable lessons:

- *Time spent playing with loved ones is time well spent.* It fosters a stronger bond and creates lasting memories. Being in the moment and being present is by far the best way to live.

- *Taking a break from work and responsibilities is essential for mental and emotional well-being.* It rejuvenates the spirit and recharges the mind. Work is a distraction from connection, family, and making memories for many of us. Find that balance of work and play.

- *Simple wins.* Embracing the simplicity of play brings joy and happiness. As adults, we sometimes forget the magic of letting go and immersing ourselves in the present moment. We get so enamored with our goals, progress, and personal development that we forget to play and just be as we are.

- *Life's purpose is not just about work and achievements.* It's also about finding joy, connection, and fulfillment in the little moments. In fact, for most of us, the achievements are fleeting and still leave us craving more. That's because we are wired for connection, hugging and touching, laughing, and playing with the ones we love.

- *Accepting invitations to play, whether from loved ones or from within us, opens doors to creativity, imagination, and a sense of purpose.* It allows us to find new pathways to love and to express joy. Opening ourselves up to play allows us to live the life we deserve.

Will my son remember that specific day? I don't know; probably not. Will I? *Yes.* I will remember it forever because it is one of the days where he inspired me and challenged me to grow. All because I accepted the invitation to play.

## WORK VERSUS PLAY

The British philosopher Alan Watts had a lecture about work and play in which he acknowledged how we make an arbitrary division between them, saying, "You are supposed to work in order to earn enough money to give you sufficient leisure time for something entirely different called *having fun* or *play.* And this is the most ridiculous division of things because everything that we do, however tough it is, however strenuous, can be turned into the same kind of play as I was showing you—and I was completely fascinated with spinning that orange around my head."[4] If we are committed to the idea of *work* with no *play*, each one of us will be stressed, unfulfilled, and not whole. Healing means wholeness; that is why our souls are screaming at us to find adventure and create more joy and fun. The invitation is for us to choose vocations and a life that bring us fun and joy. Living the life you deserve is hardly about the degrees or your illusion of independence; most people who brag about the two are empty and looking for validation and acceptance. Allow yourself to play. Allow adventure and wandering to take you where they will. Continue to have a lust for life. Allow yourself, from this point forward, to build a life where the lines of play and work are so blurred that it's all the same.

I couldn't tell you how many hours per week or how many days per week that I "work." To me, it's all the same. I engage everything now with the same essence and vigor.

I look at my responsibility as a father as fun—it's not about being serious and strict. Yes, I teach my kids boundaries and respect and to strive for individual greatness. I also teach them to have fun, to laugh a lot, to be random, and to adventure through life.

The first month I made $100,000 was the most stressful month of my life. I didn't even enjoy something that less than 1 percent of people in the world experience because I was so focused on releasing my course, doing it right, and being mistake-free with the release. When I did that, I was in the essence of seriousness and forcing things. I was so focused on production that I did indeed create the outcome, but as a deliberate creator, I focused only on the *end* and not how I would *feel*.

About two years went by before I had a similar opportunity. This time, because of that interlude with my son where we played hooky from daycare, my energy was totally different. After integrating a more playful mindset to balance out my determination and seriousness, I did it again: I made $100,000 in one month. Unlike before, I wasn't keeping close track of how much I was making. I felt lighter—and in fact I was. My actual body weight decreased when I started looking at life as play. This time, I had a joyous, uninhibited, "evil villain" laugh—like the Joker in the *Batman* movie—and shrugged my shoulders back and forth as I danced, jumped, and tapped my feet together. I frolicked into the kitchen and ate a plum and put some Tajin on a mango—that's how I celebrated one of my greatest financial achievements.

*This is the real secret of life—to be completely engaged*
*with what you are doing in the here and now. And*
*instead of calling it work, realize that it is play.*[5]

— **Alan Watts,** *The Essence of Alan Watts*

# JOURNAL PROMPTS:
# JOY

- What brings you the most joy right now in your life?

- For the thing/people/place that you name, how much of your time are you currently spending there?

- Is there something you want to experience that you think will bring you joy?

- Do you have any rituals now to acknowledge and honor joy, success, and when good things happen to you?

- Reflect on a recent moment of gratitude that brought you immense joy. How did it make you feel, and how can you cultivate more gratitude in your daily life?

- Think about a hobby or activity that has brought you pure joy in the past. How can you make more time to prioritize your happiness and incorporate this activity into your life?

- Consider the people who bring you joy and uplift your spirits. Who are they? Reflect on ways to strengthen your connections and nurture these relationships to further enhance your happiness.

- Imagine a future version of yourself living a life filled with joy and fulfillment. What does that life look like? Take a moment to envision your ideal state of happiness and outline some actionable steps you can take to work toward manifesting that vision.

The biggest change I made in my adult life was giving myself genuine permission to feel joy. I fell deeper in love with my life once I said, "I deserve to feel joy and not only when I earn it or do something great but even on my bad days, even when I feel like I'm not trending in the direction I need to go in." Permitting yourself to feel joy keeps you going on the days when your mood dips. Joy gets you back to alignment and your discipline. Joy gets you back to the fun and gratitude. Joy gets you back to that youthful energy that keeps us alive and well.

— **Sylvester McNutt III**, *Live the Life You Deserve*

I need everyone to understand that societies built on capitalism need their citizens to think that their worth is solely about how much money they make and how much they produce. Its function is to dehumanize them. That is why you are tired. That is why you're out of alignment. That is why you feel like you don't belong. Get back to the things that make you *you*. Get back to simply being a human. Get back to the community, to fun, to joy, to telling stories around the fire and making memories.

— **Sylvester McNutt III**, *Live the Life You Deserve*

This society makes it seem like your value is to work, pay a bunch of bills, and then die. We must mentally escape this system. Life is meant to be enjoyed. We are meant to watch sunsets and dance to music. We are meant to laugh with those we love and get comfort when we need to cry. We are here to share love through the summer and snuggle in the winters. Life is meant to be savored.

— **Sylvester McNutt III,** *Live the Life You Deserve*

You are not working this hard just to pay bills and die. Give yourself permission to have as much fun as you need, to have hobbies that take up time and give you meaning. If you work at a job, be sure to use all your sick, vacation, and days off. If you drop dead tomorrow, that job will have you replaced the next day. If you work for yourself, get out of a scarcity mindset and give yourself time off. Even if you love your job, give yourself the time off you deserve to feel and see the other pieces of life.

— **Sylvester McNutt III,** *Live the Life You Deserve*

Some people say, "Don't take yourself too seriously because you don't get out of here alive." Some people say, "Take everything seriously and become successful." The answer for you can be in the middle of those and can sway as your life desires and needs change. Give yourself permission to enjoy life.

— **Sylvester McNutt III,** *Live the Life You Deserve*

## CHAPTER 9

# INTEGRATING RITUALS OF PLAY, ABUNDANCE, AND JOY

So much of our life lies within our daily habits; however, there is a deeper and richer viewpoint that can change all our lives for the better. As society moves faster and faster, it's important to have rituals that slow us down, heal us, and bring us into communion with the life we want to live. In this chapter, we accept the invitation to integrate rituals of play, abundance, and joy.

I am a deliberate creator of my experience, and there is more than enough for me. I never feel cheated. I never feel lack. I don't have enemies. Nobody is here to hurt me. Most people who get to know me love me. I think it terms of abundance, and I am always mindful that I am a conscious creator of my life.

— **Sylvester McNutt III,** *Live the Life You Deserve*

I deserve to feel joy, and I deserve to play, daily. I find joy in simple activities like listening to music, eating real food at a slow pace, being in community, frolicking through nature, and writing what is on my soul. I can never go broke because I am rich in soul and spirit, which is energy. I deserve to feel joy and choose a playful energy whenever I want. If you accept and honor your own journey, you'll see that you too deserve this same mindset and energy.

— **Sylvester McNutt III,** *Live the Life You Deserve*

I'm writing to you with a smile on my face from ear to ear and my eyes brimming with tears. Tears of joy, of happiness. They won't drop yet because I won't let them until I write my last letter to you. I look at each chapter as a love letter and the book as a journal.

The smile ignited on my face because of an interaction with a stranger online that took me back to a memory that I wish I could feel again—a memory of abundance, joy, and play. Eight months ago, I left a comment on a YouTube video expressing how much joy I had listening to a particular song, one that my father used to listen to when I was a young boy. I'd been listening to it on a night when I was missing him, missing my childhood, and missing the innocence that we had as children. I have a vivid memory of my father playing his music at the highest possible volume. My mother didn't always love it, and she would plead to him to turn it down, but when he was in party mode, there was only one volume: as loud as possible.

He had two big towers for speakers, and each one had a 12-inch subwoofer on the lower part, plus a smaller speaker above it that blasted the midrange and treble notes. They sat inside of an oak-finished wooden box that was about five feet tall. When my father would play his music, the house would shake and tremble, and my body would be transported to the studio where the musicians performed every note. To this day, I have never met another person whose music station could rival my father's. He kept up with the times through his lifetime. He had the disks that you could play, then tape cassettes, then CDs. Toward the end of his life, he owned an iPod and plugged it in to his speakers to play his music. A gift of a Bluetooth-connected speaker would've been something that he loved.

One night in the early '90s, my father was playing one of his favorite musicians at the time, Whodini. I swear I heard their smash hit "Friends" more times than they did. As the music played through our walls, he'd grab me by the hands, and we danced and bounced to the beat. We sang the song back to each other like we created it; we embodied the music like it was ours. For the rest of the night, my father would put on a concert. He would say, "You're too young for this, but I need you to hear this good music. Music is for the soul. It's a tool to make you feel joy, to make you think deeply, to let you feel that you are alive." His music was cultured and spanned many generations; he'd play Etta James, James Brown, or Sam Cooke. Due to the varied people he met during his time in the Army, he picked up pieces of popular and obscure music available outside of our neighborhood too.

Whenever we think of the past, we must remember that they simply weren't as connected as we are today. They didn't have social media and cellphones. Discovering new albums and music was a way to discover abundance. It often led our parents and grandparents to moments of joy and play. The path and practice of discovering new music even led a lot of our ancestors to find purpose, to find a reason to live, to find themselves.

My father's vocation and passion was culinary, but something that brought him great joy was music—listening to it, savoring it, and sharing his discoveries with people he loved. I know that the night I'm referring to was a Saturday night because he would say, "On Saturday, we go to the disco." *Disco* is sort of an outdated word now in American culture, but in the 1970s it was both a style of music and a club or party where people would go listen to popular music.

For my father, Sunday was about church, a big family-style breakfast, and Chicago Bears football. Saturday was about chores, being outside all day playing and living, and going to the disco at night. I didn't know when I was living it, but my father was the first person to introduce me and my family to rituals of the heart, to rituals that made us whole, to rituals that brought us together. These rituals covered us for the entire weekend as we could all find joy, abundance, and play.

On the weekends, I never heard my father talk about work. Perhaps he did in conversations I wasn't a part of—those with other adults—but I never heard him complain about bills, opportunities or lack thereof, or his own problems. Most men from that era and before were like that. They just went to work and did whatever it took to feed the mouths they were responsible for.

As a parent, I've changed that routine slightly; I will talk to my son about my problems because I want to give him a framework for working through whatever will arise for him in the future. I want him to see that I'm equipped with the tools to handle whatever is necessary. I don't want him to think that he has problems but his dad never did. Nope, I have way more problems than you, son, but I will show you how to bring them into your vessel and heal them.

One of the best ways to do this, son, is to play. Play in your house and at work. Play in your relationships and as you wander through life. When you want to complain and stress, turn to play and joy. When you are on a date with someone, commit to play and presence. Do not interpret play as an invitation to avoid, to run, or to be irresponsible; you know we cannot do that as deliberate creators of our reality. No. For us, play is about a full integration into our lives, especially for we who have been sold the idea of seriousness as a path to fulfillment.

If you hate chores and cleaning, it could be because your mindset around it is one of duty and responsibility, one that doesn't amount to anything. Or maybe it feels like a punishment—or maybe in your household it *was* an actual punishment, so now as an adult you engage cleaning with a veneer of disdain. What if you looked at it as something joyful instead? Imagine what it would be like to have a cleaning outfit and a music playlist that hyped you up?

If you are an athlete, odds are that you don't like practice and enjoy the games much more. A lot of the athletes that I knew were this way, and that's because the games are graded and are about production. We value the outcomes of things that parallel production, especially if said production is in alignment with the life we seek. The invitation here is to recognize the day-to-day activities like cleaning, like practice, like a daily walk as *play* that will improve your mood, your energy, and your engagement with the journey. The consequences of each, I would imagine, is an actual better performance if that is truly the goal.

Of course, we could go on and on and pick many different situations or components of a process that we look at as damning, taxing, and negative. The shift for all of us to consider is:

*Can I change my perception here?*

*Can I look at this situation in a more playful way?*

*Is there healthy space for me to be more playful
in my mindset and attitude here?*

*Would being more playful make this easier?*

*Would being more playful here actually benefit me when an
element of production or grading was prevalent and present?*

The next time you are going through something deep, don't waste your time overthinking solutions; just go play. Go for a walk. Go dance in the rain. Go stretch at the park. Pull out your notebook and play with words. Sing your songs off-key and rap offbeat. Go make your favorite meal in the kitchen and make a mess. It's not avoidance, and it's not that you are running from the problems. Our solutions are often not inside of thinking and more thinking. Often, they are in the meditative states of play and wandering. Go play, and the path will find you.

— **Sylvester McNutt III,** *Live the Life You Deserve*

Stop judging your voice when you sing. Stop judging your rhythm when you dance. You're not on an audition for a talent show. Play is what we need to feel alive. Dance, sing, and judge yourself less. You deserve to have fun too.

— **Sylvester McNutt III,** *Live the Life You Deserve*

Love is created in the energy of playfulness and joy. Love is created by being present, and I mean being all the way there. Put your phone down, check your b.s. at the door, and look someone in the eye until you both can see each other's soul without the masks that society has given to us all.

— **Sylvester McNutt III,** *Live the Life You Deserve*

Relationships are simple: make sure you are fun, make sure you enjoy who you are, and create a vessel to enjoy and value the person who is directly in front of you. Don't overthink anything; stay fully present. It works every single time.

— **Sylvester McNutt III,** *Live the Life You Deserve*

If the only input you have is American entrepreneurs, then the message you receive will be to chase money, to grind, and to make everything in life about work. That might work for you, but the odds are that you want more out of life than that. Close your eyes and revisit your childhood. Imagine yourself playing and that all those things that you see are what you need to add to your plate as well. Yes, jumping over the imaginary lava, building a tent, and flying in your spaceship. Don't ever stop dreaming. Keep pretending and playing, as these activities will truly make you feel alive.

— **Sylvester McNutt III,** *Live the Life You Deserve*

At your funeral, they won't talk about your job. They are going to talk about what you did to make them feel alive. They will talk about the times you were present in their lives and how you shifted the way they think. They will mention the fun, goofy, and silly times that were filled with laughter and joy. Have fun in life because none of us are getting out of here alive. Go play, allow joy in, and thrive because you deserve it.

— **Sylvester McNutt III,** *Live the Life You Deserve*

# WHY I NEVER WORRY

Sometimes we suffer because we think we need to approach everything in life with a great deal of seriousness. As a person who used to be serious about everything, I promise you there's a happier life that awaits you when you learn to play, joke around, and enjoy the little moments in life. Never remove the element of playfulness from your life, for it is that youthfulness that keeps us alive and well.

These are the reasons I never worry—and you shouldn't either.

### Most things don't matter that much.

Ninety-nine percent of the things we worry about don't matter when we view the bigger picture of our lives. Sometimes, the worry is misplaced and is an inappropriate emotion that should be allowed to pass. The worry is often fear about fear. One of the mechanisms of worry is that it magnifies potential problems.

### Fear is normal.

I am okay with being afraid, and you should be too. Fear is an emotion, and once you choose to live an authentic life, you accept that fear is a normal component of the human experience, and it is necessary for survival. Trying to "get rid" of fear, in my opinion, is the wrong path. I'm afraid to write books, but I'm going to do it anyway. I was afraid to be a parent, but I'm going to do it the best way I can. I was afraid the first time I tried to earn $100k in a month, but I went for it anyway. I used to fear asking girls out when I was 18, but I did it anyway. Fear is not a red light. It's an invitation.

**I am a deliberate creator of my experience, and there is more than enough for me.**

I never feel cheated. I never feel lack. I don't have enemies. Nobody is here to hurt me. Most people who get to know me love me. I think in terms of abundance, and I am always mindful that I am a conscious creator of my life.

**I deserve to feel joy, and I deserve to play, daily.**

I find joy in simple activities like listening to music, eating real food at a slow pace, being in community, frolicking through nature, and writing what is on my soul. I can never go broke because I am rich in soul and spirit, which is energy. I deserve to feel joy and choose a playful energy whenever I want.

If you accept and honor your own journey, you'll see that you too deserve this same mindset and energy. The consequence of this energy is that you will play and feel joy.

# THE DIFFERENCE BETWEEN GOALS, HABITS, ROUTINES, AND RITUALS

We are at an interesting crossroads in human existence, where billions of people across the world are simply looking for balance. Some people work a job from sunup to sundown and only have Sundays off. Some people are working two or three jobs. Some people are stressed and overwhelmed and are looking for a pathway to release the pressure of life. Some parents love being parents but simply don't get enough time to themselves. At the end of the day, no matter who we are or what we are currently doing, thriving for most of us can simply mean finding balance.

It appears to me that most humans thrive when life is simple and organized, when we have conflicts that we feel confident we can resolve or learn from, and most importantly when we exist inside of some community. It appears that we thrive when our basic needs are meet and satisfied physically, culturally, mentally, and emotionally. (This is when we've got the bottom four levels of Maslow's pyramid taken care of so we can strive for the top.)

I've seen a lot of content and books lately about setting goals as a result of so many of us seeking balance. Achieving goals seems to have become the be-all and end-all of finding balance, success, and purpose within. Within the last decade, social media has led Americans to think of goals as a "thing" to acquire. We have all heard phrases like "relationship goals," denoting that the perceived image of what other people have is an objective for ourselves.

So, are goals the most important thing when we are looking to create and design the life we want? When I first started writing this book, I would've told you yes, and that is because I was brainwashed to believe I needed to define my effort in relation to a particular point. Now, my thought is more nuanced and spacious.

I like to think of this like a student who signed up for a martial art. When you first start off, you're a novice. There are some targets or goals that you must hit in order to understand the landscape of the discipline, and once you hit said goals, they will take you deep into the space of mastery. But goals won't help you become a black belt. Nope. Goals, after a while, might not even motivate or inspire you. Once you are on the path of mastery, goals sort of fall off, and it graduates to another phase. That's when we can introduce habits, routines, and rituals.

I shared this framework with my private mastermind, The Mastery Circle, and it moved mountains for all of us once we integrated the framework into our individual realms. Rituals, routines, and habits are related concepts, but they have distinct differences in terms of their nature and purpose:

- *Rituals:* Rituals are characterized by their symbolic and ceremonial nature. They feel deeper and more impactful to the soul or psyche. They involve actions performed in a specific order or for a specific reason, often accompanied by meaningful gestures, words, or objects. Rituals are usually associated with family; relationships; or cultural, religious, or spiritual practices and can hold deep emotional or symbolic significance. They are often done to mark important events and transitions or to create a sense of connection and meaning. Examples of rituals include wedding ceremonies, religious observances, and cultural celebrations.[1]

- *Routines:* Routines are a series of actions or tasks that are performed regularly and in a specific order. Routines focus more on efficiency, organization, and structure in daily life. They provide a sense of predictability and help individuals manage their time and responsibilities. Routines can encompass various aspects of life, such as morning, work, gym, and bedtime routines. While routines can be flexible, they are typically designed to bring consistency and stability to daily activities.[2]

- *Habits:* Habits are behaviors that have become automatic and ingrained over time through repetition. They are actions that individuals perform with little conscious thought. Habits can be positive or negative and are often formed due to consistent repetition of behavior in a particular context. For example, brushing your teeth before bed or checking your phone as soon as you wake up are habits. Habits are closely related to the brain's reward system and are typically formed through a cue, routine, and reward cycle.[3]

There are a bunch of different rituals that will be passed to us from our family, our society, our culture, our religion, or a spiritual practice. To respect the boundary of time, I'm going to share with you two rituals that I love. One is a yearly ritual that was passed to me by my family. The other is a weekly ritual that I created that powers my week, and it's something I look forward to every Sunday.

## MY YEARLY RITUAL AND WHY RITUALS NEED TO BE OUR FOCUS

I love my birthday (August 23), and every single year I'll celebrate. My celebrations have been different throughout the years. I've traveled outside the country, I've traveled to a different city, I've been on road trips within my state, I've taken a cruise, and I've gotten an Airbnb in the jungle. This year, I am going up to Sonoma, California, to run a six-mile race, go to expensive restaurants, and drink wine.

Next year, who knows? I may end up back in South America or maybe Africa. Japan sounds nice, and Spain is calling me now. It's even possible that I'll simply stay in Arizona and have people over at the house. No matter where I am or who I'm with, whether it's an abundance of people or I'm by myself, I have a commitment to celebrate my birthday.

When I come across people who don't celebrate their birthdays, I always ask why. A lot of times, I hear their birthdays were overlooked in their youth. The empath in me suffers when I hear that. However, I know that my responsibility is not to hold on to the sadness but instead to invite the person sharing that story with me to the great ritual of *celebrating yourself.*

The first thing necessary to understand regarding self-celebration is that it isn't even about me. No, I've adopted the mindset that my birthday is a moment to understand the great sacrifices that my parents, their parents, and their parents' parents made for me. My birthday is a moment to reflect on the great generations of people who created me and held space for me to hold this space. Celebrating my birthday is no longer solely about me; I owe it to them to celebrate life.

You and I, as we stand here today, are a testament to the work of generations and generations of people before us. We owe it to them to honor their excellence and their spirit and all the sacrifices that they made for us to be thriving in life. Even if we thrive every single day, it is still our duty to have some moment of self-celebration that will honor all the people who came before as well as ourselves in this present moment. I don't want this invitation to sound heavy when I write it; it doesn't sound heavy to me. In fact, it feels freeing.

If your birthday was overlooked because it was near another holiday and you hold on to the upset of never being celebrated fully the way you deserved, I understand.

It's possible that your parents didn't mean to diminish your importance but may have had to because of limited resources. Most of us have had to find a way to make things work with the resources that we had. If you can look back and see great holiday experiences that your parents tried to cultivate for all of you, well, it's easier to be understanding if you can see where your parents had to make sacrifices.

Now let's look at it from a different perspective: maybe your parents didn't celebrate you and your birthday because they didn't know how to *celebrate themselves.* It's that classic tale of how we can't expect something from someone that they don't give to themselves. When you hear that, I don't want you to get feel anger and resentment toward your parents. I want you to understand that they simply couldn't give it to themselves—and maybe that came from your grandparents and further generations back.

Whatever the reason, we're not here to place blame; that is not our mission. Our objective here is simply to deploy empathy and curiosity so we can understand that we do not have to take it personally when we were not celebrated. If these words are resonating with you, it means that it's time to *celebrate yourself.*

So, what I want you to do is to start planning for your birthday. And planning does not have to be extravagant, but it can be. If you want to take a cruise, you should. If you've never left your state or the country, you should. If you want to go to the fanciest restaurant in your town that you don't think you can afford today, well, then create a vision of you sitting in that restaurant, eating the best meal possible. I promise that once you choose to be a delivery creator of the birthday and self-celebration experience that you want to feel, life will conspire to make that happen.

As a matter of fact, I'll do this with you right now. This book will be released on my birthday. I believe that for me to have a successful book release, I'm going to need to be at home. I feel the most grounded when I am at home. So, what I'm going to do is make sure that I celebrate my birthday for the whole month. At the top of the month of August, I will travel internationally, just like I am doing as I write now. In the second half of the month, I will go home so I am grounded for my birthday. Then, leading into September, I will travel again to spend time with friends, family, and hopefully you.

Boom—there it is. I don't need to be more specific than that as a deliberate creator because I just know I am going to use next August to release the best book of my life. Travel is already lighting me up. Putting my goals, dreams, and energy to the universe is creating an earthquake of energy that will help me make this easier and easier. I named the country Spain. Watch, someone from Spain will contact me to let me know that I can stay at their place, that they can be a tour guide, or that they'll help me getting in and out of the country. My trip just became 30x easier just because of self-celebration through the vessel of deliberate creation.

"Okay. But, Sylvester, I don't have a book releasing, so how can I do this?" Well, don't assume that my megaphone or anyone else's is more powerful than yours. We are both deliberate creators. How about this: write me on social media and tell me what you are doing for your birthday, tell me where the party is going to be, tell me what museum we are going to, or tell me what workout class we are hitting. You never know—I may join. Then, tell your best friend right now. Don't ask permission either. Just say, "Here's what we are doing for my birthday next year," and list it out with a powerful emotion behind it. And then from there, tell your co-workers and tell the barista the next time you order coffee. What you'll notice are synchronicities happening.

Let's say you name that you want to visit a particular restaurant. After you declare this, you may be on a bus or walking down the street, and randomly you'll see a server from that restaurant, noticing the logo on her shirt as she gets into a car. Let's say you want to do something like bake a cake at home and spend time in the company of loved ones. Coincidentally, your high school best friend will be in town, your favorite co-workers will be available, and the one friend who never has money will have enough to come. It happens every single time with my friends, and it all starts with us accepting the invitation to self-celebrate every year.

"What if I don't want to party or have dinner, and I simply want to go to work or just sit back and relax?" My answer is simple: do what is most authentic to you. Just make sure that your choice truly is authentic, and it is not laced in unworthiness or some older story about why you shouldn't be able to celebrate. If you're stoic and simple and celebration for you is a content, "Hey, I made it," I'm good with that as long as that is genuinely who you are and not a wound or outdated paradigm speaking on your behalf. Make sense?

## MY WEEKLY RITUAL AND WHY

If you feel uneasy, unsettled, chaotic, or even stressed, a grounding ritual is the remedy. I thrive best when I move slowly and do activities that are important to me and those around me. I've cultivated these rituals that I do almost every Sunday, and they give me the energy I need to thrive and live the life I deserve.

This ritual allows me to be inside grounded and calm energy. I do this every week as an anchor, as a space to ground me, to serve the soul, mind, and body. My root chakra is always activated on Sunday as I have dedicated that day to grounding, security, and inner safety.

### *Sunday Rituals that Give Me Organization, Joy, and Abundance*

- **Slow morning start:** Yerba mate tea, coffee, water, vitamins. Meditation, prayer, or fun conversation with my family. Music or comedy videos as ambiance. Going for a walk, making the bed, and doing my hygiene routine.

- **Middle-of-the-morning workout:** Lifting, running, stretching. If none of those feel right, then a one- to two-hour walk.

- **Deep self-care routine:** Shower, wash and exfoliate the face, wash and condition my beard, and wash my hair followed by an at-home spa, in which I soak my feet, clip my nails, and cut my hair if needed. I'll do a face mask, snack on a homemade fresh fruit platter, sip wine or water, and usually sit with my kids so they witness the self-care and participate.

- **Clean office:** During the week, I spend the most time at home in my office. I refuse to walk into a dirty "workspace" on Monday morning, so on Sunday, I take the time to clean the desk, monitors, keyboards, and whiteboards and vacuum the carpet. During this process, I also journal on how I want the week to go and what I want to accomplish. I write my goals on the whiteboard at the top of the week and rewrite them every day-ish.

- **Slow dinner in community:** This is easily the best way to end a Sunday. Sometimes, it's me alone or with friends or family. The emphasis for me is that it is *slow*. I have no preference if we go out to dinner or if we make it. I can be cooked for or I can cook. Again, the emphasis is that it is slow and about community, and no one is wasting the time on their cellphone.

# JOURNAL PROMPTS:
# PLAY!

- What is one habit you have that you take very seriously? How can you incorporate fun into it?

- Do you think you *deserve* joy? Why or why not?

- Do you feel like a deliberate creator of your experience? Can you create a life of more joy and play for yourself?

- Think of your weekly routine. Is there a way to include a ritual to help ground the energy of your week as you begin or end it?

- Let's assume that you see the need for more joy and play in your life. However, you are telling yourself the story of how busy you are, how tired you are, and how much further you need to go. What do you think will be the lever that moves the needle of your life? Will focusing on the overwhelm give you more joy or will focusing on the joy give you less overwhelm? What do you want to believe?

- Kids wake up and think about play and for the most part appear to radiate joy. Adults wake up and think about bills, why we are not enough, and our wounds. Is it possible that being more childlike will heal you, inspire you, and push you into the life that you deserve? Journal more on why you deserve play.

Make play a big component of your life. The idea that everything needs to be serious, deep, and dark is an outdated paradigm. Sure, life is hard at times for all. But we all deserve to play. Have a reverence for your soul, as it needs to play. Allow play to be a part of your life daily, and I promise you will thrive.

— **Sylvester McNutt III,** *Live the Life You Deserve*

Most people are going to suffer greatly if their life is only about working, paying bills, and chasing the next level. Life is not the corporate ladder. You are here to frolic in nature, to spend hours laughing with loved ones, and to chase your curiosities.

— **Sylvester McNutt III,** *Live the Life You Deserve*

If you feel like the second half of your life is flying by, it's because you are living the same day repeatedly. Lean in to the idea of being spontaneous instead of always having a plan. Fall in love with the idea that you are still safe even when off the plan, that you are worthy of living a full life even if things on the "to-do" list go unchecked. This is your life, and while we do need habits, routines, and security, we also need those spontaneous nights with people we'll never forget.

— **Sylvester McNutt III,** *Live the Life You Deserve*

I need everyone to understand that once you make something an option, it is no longer a priority. We each have limited energies and time, so be mindful of what you make an option and what you make a priority. Abundance should always be a priority. Don't think of abundance as just money or wealth because it's so much more. Abundance is about the bandwidth of your healing, it is about the capacity of your possibilities, and it is about the unlimited love that radiates through your soul. Whenever you think about the depths of the wells, make sure you recognize that they are always full for you.

— **Sylvester McNutt III,** *Live the Life You Deserve*

CHAPTER 10

# THE ART OF DETACHMENT AND NOT FORCING

Suffering occurs inside when we think we are owed. We believe in entitlement, and we try to force what is not. Detachment allows you to thrive. Detachment allows you to flow and meander through life. But there's a duality here, because if we are seeking the love life, the career, and the health we want, then isn't there a great deal of effort and energy? Isn't it best to be in energetic alignment with the outcome we seek?

Well, you've gathered that this far into the book, we must learn and make space for detachment as well as attachment. Both dualities help us gain leverage as we dance through life. Let's dive in.

You must choose to be uncommon. You cannot have common thoughts and reach greatness. There are aspects of your life that need you to think bigger, bolder, and braver.

— **Sylvester McNutt III,** *Live the Life You Deserve*

With missions from the soul, we cannot think about the outcome; we cannot chase and force a particular outcome. We have to be truly present with what is, and we must allow the commitment to the mission to be the main thing.

— **Sylvester McNutt III,** *Live the Life You Deserve*

The golden tool of detachment will help you be physically lighter and feel lighter emotionally and allow you to experience more joy and inner peace. Detachment will allow you to pull back from situations, never take them personally, and observe things for what they truly are.

An invitation to detachment doesn't mean to not care about anything, to have no attachments, or to be completely numb to the world—at least that's not how I see it. In fact, the majority of what we have read about so far is about passions and habits and how we can attach to them in a healthy way. But healing means wholeness, and in order to step into our highest self, we must recognize that there is great power in detachment as a tool as well.

Detachment is a tool that you can turn on and off as you meander through life, a tool that allows you to heal and thrive when used in the right situations. If we accept that detachment is a tool rather than a state of always being detached, there is a great advantage that we can acquire on this journey. We don't have to be dogmatic here; we don't have to accept or believe in anything all the way. That is why the invitations to use a tool makes the most sense. We can apply the art of detachment only when necessary.

## THE ROLE OF ATTACHMENT AND DETACHMENT IN OUR LIVES

You can find numerous definitions and understandings of detachment in academia, religion, spiritual practices, and personal development circles. John Bowlby, the psychiatrist who pioneered attachment theory, describes in his book *Attachment* the necessity of both strong attachment and separation to develop autonomy. He writes, "The child needs to learn how to detach from the parent to be able to grow."[1]

As we age, our attachment to our parents changes, and we slowly detach from them and the "I need you in order to live" emotional hook that dominates our younger years. Bowlby describes several stages of attachment that people typically go through in which the degree and potency of one's attachment changes as the relationships evolve. A dualistic experience is occurring where we are both detaching, and the attachment is changing.

Attachment theory describes people's expected behaviors and patterns in relationships in the context of one's attachment style, which is determined by certain dimensions. Although some psychologists describe three or four dimensions, one of the most common systems uses just two: anxiety and avoidance.[2] Entire books have been written about attachment theory, so I won't go in depth here. Suffice it to say that understanding your own attachment style can help you on your path of self-mastery and connect with others in safer, more authentic ways.

Depending on your religion and your upbringing, you may have heard that having a connection with God is the best way—or maybe even the only way—to have a good life. I took a world religion class my senior year of college and was completely overwhelmed with the robust information and stories that were shared with us. The professor who taught the class was an encyclopedia of knowledge. One day, he said to us, "You were each raised a particular way based on your parents' beliefs. But in this class, I want to teach you about many modern-day religions, their origins, how they have evolved, and some key principles of them. You will also hear how religion has shaped societies that no longer exist. Knowing about how other people think will help you become better citizens of the world. You will be better parents, partners, and friends."

Every single day I had a headache from the overload of information in that class—and that's not hyperbole. That's a realistic reflection of the time. I failed the class in the worst way, but I do remember leaving class that semester with this thought: *People like to attach to ideas. Some ideas and our attachment to them can free us, empower us; for some people, attachment is the very reason they will perish.*

Simple.

Deep.

Still, that thought has never left me: people like to attach to ideas.

## DETACH FROM HONOR CULTURE

We see attachments play out in the form of identity politics, in the pride people have for their culture, country, and even sports teams. We have all seen people physically fighting or arguing with people online over their attachment to a sports team. This is because we live in an honor culture.

I was first introduced to this term in an NPR podcast called *Hidden Brain*, in the episode "Made of Honor." The main speaker for this documentary was Ryan Brown, social scientist and professor at Rice University. The host of the show, Shankar Vedantam, holds the space for us to learn from these experts weekly.

In the podcast episode, Ryan explained an honor culture as "societies that put the defensive reputation at the center of social life and make that defense one of the highest priorities that people have." He shared two stories as examples: In the case of one famous soccer player, his sister's virtue had been called into question by an opponent, and he felt he absolutely had to respond with aggression by calling him names and going chest-to-chest with him. In another story of racing motorcycles from his child-hood, Ryan described how excessive risk-taking behavior was meant to build your reputation and to show how brave and tough you are. Ryan also explained what produces honor cultures:

> The conditions that social scientists believe spawn honor cultures fall into really two main categories. The first is that, economically, people must feel insecure. That kind of insecurity at an economic level often co-incides with poverty. But it's more than just poverty. It's the instability. You've got to feel uncertain about whether you will survive economically the next season, the next year. And combined with that economic insecurity, there's a sense of the unreliability of law enforcement. So, what we refer to as the rule of law is not very strong. When these two things coincide that makes threats, social threats, especially important. If somebody comes and steals your cattle, threatened your family, you know that nobody's coming to save you, that's it for you. And so, reputation is incredibly important. You want to have a reputation as someone that nobody should mess with. They're going to think twice before messing with you, or your stuff, or your family. Because they know that you're going to respond aggressively and violently. And that sort of reputation protects you.[3]

Do you remember that story I described in Chapter 4 about how the boy James attacked me during the *Killer-man* football game? Well, I came from an honor culture, and my going back to the yard prepared to fight him was under the banner of honor. When I first wrote that story in the book, I wrote it as a hero's arc in which I as the protagonist had to overcome an inner weakness and defeat an external conflict. After I beat him up, I gained respect within the neighborhood as people witnessed me in my highest strength.

Now let's add another layer to the story. For any of us who have been in a situation like that, we can ask ourselves questions to lead us on the path of genuine introspection. Considering these concepts is the first step toward recognizing where you are attached to our honor culture and beginning the process of detaching.

- Am I going to this fight because of honor and pride?

- Is the fight going to be worth defending my honor and pride?

- Is it possible that I can detach from this honor and pride?

- Is it possible that I can let go of these situations and just move forward?

- Is it possible that vengeance is not a solution?

- Is it possible that letting go is the best choice?

- Do I have to fight and stand up for myself in this moment?

When I interviewed Traver Boehm, the men's coach and founder of the UNcivilized Men's Movement, he said that "men need to be dangerous, but we shouldn't be a danger."[4] This sort of line encompasses the totality of integration; it encompasses the ability to detach, to know that you can hurt and harm someone but choose to restrain yourself, to not do it. One day, my son may be in the same situation I was in as a kid, and I don't want to instill honor culture in him. I would like to teach him to detach from honor culture so he can make the best decisions for himself in that moment. A detachment from honor culture gives us access to a tightened sense of self and confidence within our ability to see the truth. Most importantly, it allows us to recognize safety and danger and keeps us closer to choosing safety.

If you are reading this within the U.S., then you already know that a major component of the honor culture that we have all been conditioned to believe is that we must attain success through the American dream. The modern American psyche is rooted in capitalism, its skeleton is based off the industrial revolution, and its flesh is consumerism and finding personal worth in your job title. This is why the modern American psyche is so broken—none of this is real. Coupled with our addictions to sugar, fake food, politics, and conflict, it's easy to see why most Americans are suffering. It has been designed this way. They want us to be fat, lazy, and broke because those populations are easy to control. The powers that be are extremely predatory in nature, and that is why so many of us feel attacked and marginalized, like we are fighting these uphill battles.

This shouldn't be surprising. You can go back into American history, from modern times to its earliest days, and see that this society has been founded on rape, murder, war, exploitations, and extractions. Each person born in America is inheriting generational gifts and generational trauma. We live on stolen land, *and* we live in a space that uses us for extractions. We live in a place where morality is based on profit.

A process of detachment, to some degree, is necessary if you live here; otherwise, you will be controlled and you will suffer. Detachment from some aspects of the honor culture of the U.S. is necessary to find your authentic self. Here's what I discovered in my own journey:

- *Detach my self-worth from my job:* In my journey, I had to detach from the idea that my human worth was wrapped up in my career choice, something we particularly condition men to believe. Taking that pressure off me allowed me to get out of a career that I was in only for money. It allowed me to come here, to writing books, to a vocation that makes my soul feel alive.

- *Detach from society's imposed labels:* Another conversation that I had to leave from an honor culture perspective is that I am a "minority." That term, to me, has psychological warfare tactics laced into it as it is literally describing something as minor. I stopped describing myself as a minority, and I'm simply Sylvester.

- *Detach from superficial "culture":* Lastly, I broke up with the part of the culture here that is obsessed with politics, the news, celebrities, and fake foods. Those parts of our culture, to me, rob me of my joy and peace, and they rob me of the ability to connect with others on a genuine level.

Now, that's just for me. Your journey might be different; your society and culture may be different. For you to thrive, however, there are parts of an honor culture's conditioning that you'll have to question and challenge. This can seem "offensive" to people you share the cultures with. It can seem like you don't value or appreciate the culture, but that's far from the truth.

Our duty is to move society forward. Each one of us. We cannot do that if we blindly accept what is, if we never challenge what is, if we do not try to make it better. Sylvester is not making the world a better place if he argues about politics, but you might; that's why this conversation isn't one of judgment.

My brother and father were both in the U.S. military. My cousin and grandfather were both police officers in Illinois, vocations full of honor that are about loyalty and a commitment to a mission. They are vocations that do not align with my soul and my path, even though that is what I come from.

Perhaps through your vocation, through your calling, you reimagine your culture's food to showcase it to the world in a different light. You might reinterpret a meat-heavy cuisine in a vegan style, for instance. This is not you disrupting tradition; this is you detaching from what was so you can use your creativity to explore what can be.

Now we are starting to see the power of duality, the power of detaching, so we can have space to find our way. It's the power of being aware when an honor culture's condition is present.

## THE ART OF DETACHMENT IN PARTNERSHIP

A few years back, I was coaching a guy whose sole mission was to get his ex-girlfriend back. Zack wanted her, and he wanted her bad. The thought of becoming one again with her consumed his day-to-day. They dated for two years in college, and after graduation they both went on to do their master's degrees at different schools. She went to University of Southern California, and he went to the University of Miami. They didn't have a breakup that was rooted in bad blood or bad times; they had the ideal relationship but chose to study in different places.

Zack hired me to be his coach after moving back Los Angeles, California. His objectives for me were help getting his girl back, help him stay organized, and hold him accountable to his integrity and goals. Keeping someone in line with their goals and integrity is easy; that's a skill I've mastered as a coach. Helping you get your girl back, however, is easily the biggest challenge. That result is not up to our strategy; it's up to energy, timing, the heart, the soul, God, nature, and everything other than our scripts.

He said, "I want her back. I need her back. I'm willing to do whatever it takes."

This is a hard position to be in as a coach because you can see sometimes when people are clouded with love, even when they create a reality that is not based on the present facts. Delusions are fine sometimes; they can help the process or they can hinder it. And, as a coach, one of the reasons people hire you is to also have some tablespoons of delusion with their coffee so you can help them see a world that doesn't exist quite yet. I love being a coach because it lets me dive into a world of fantasy and mysticism, and we get to play in the gray area of life.

On a personal level, the journey of "trying to get your girl back" was a wound that I felt in my own life at one point, and I vowed to never do that again. I wanted to tell him, "It's not worth it." However, I didn't feel like that would be fair to him; it was my wound talking. Fairness to him would be to check my own wounds, be objective, and use all the tools I've developed to help him in his missions. An integrated teacher must have this ability.

I told him during the onboarding process, "Hey, I want to be transparent with you. This journey brings up wounds for me. I had a time in my life where I was trying to get back with an old flame, and it didn't go my way. I'm happy now with how things have turned out, but for a while I was in a rut trying to rekindle this flame. I want you to know this from the beginning so you know what I am up against as your coach. I believe I have the skills to support you if you'd like to move forward."

He said, "You are the right coach for this job because if it doesn't work out, I know you have the empathy and strength to support me. Because I'm going to be down bad if I don't get her back!"

We laughed over the idea of him being "down bad."

### Recognize Limitations: Never Force the Medicine

I would invite all of us who are teachers, leaders, and parents to check ourselves when we are the ones who are being called on for support. We have medicine in our words and presence, but we can taint the potency if we are not aware of what we are up against. I would invite each of us to also be aware of our teacher's capability and boundaries. And, lastly, as a teacher, parent, and coach, you must learn and master the art of detachment to make your teachings more potent so your students don't suffer because you were weak.

It's possible that in school, you were a terrible student and now you have lofty expectations of your child. Odds are, you don't have the study habits, skills, or know-how to set your child up for success in this case. If so, you must be aware of how potent your medicine is. It might mean deferring to the other parent for leadership within schooling, or just flat-out being real and transparent with your kid and saying something like, "I was not the best student, and I know why. My goal is to support you in your path. Here's what I am great at supporting, and here is where I may struggle." Detaching yourself from your ego and pedestal makes you a more powerful teacher and leader. You make the space more potent, and this doesn't dilute what you do well.

Back to my first call with Zack. I said to him, "Getting your ex back is neither hard or easy; it's only about energy and timing. I want you to close your eyes. As you close your eyes, you need to listen to my voice and feel the energy in the words. Do not think about the version of her from college—your girl has evolved past who she used to be, hopefully. Do not think about the memories of the past with the expectation that they will be mirrored in the present. You must fully detach from what was while holding a great deal of reverence and respect for what was. Do not think about what was with expectations that it will be that way today or tomorrow. That chapter came and went. You are both different people even if the essence of who you were is still intact. Focus on this version of you and this version of her. The past, especially a good past, is always there to make us smile, but you need to be present, you need to be here, you need to be in this moment with her, and she needs to be forever present with you. Do I have your commitment that mentally you will approach this from a detachment perspective?"

After I spoke to him a few minutes and aligned his energy, Zack said, "I'm so scared to ask her out, but I know that is what I want to do. How do I approach it?"

I said, "Detach from thinking. Don't think about this or that. Don't think about rejection or planning every little detail. Thinking isn't something you need here because this is a feeling you are after; a feeling is guiding you. This is a mission from the soul. With missions from the soul, we cannot think about the outcome; we cannot chase and force a particular outcome. We have to be truly present with what is, and we must allow the commitment to the mission to be the main thing.

"When we hang up, I want you to call her. Do not think or plan the call. If you are nervous, good—that means you can be authentic. Don't ask her out. Tell her you are taking her out. Paint an image of the experience. She wants to go out with you—assume that. Assume that she will fall for you. Assume that she is yours but remain detached from the assumption."

He cut me off. "What if she has a boyfriend or something right now?"

I said, "That's none of your business. If she does, she will tell you, and hell, she might have boyfriend and still might not tell you. That is none of your business. You want her, so you must create the vessel for her to come home. You haven't spoken to her in years, so whatever she has now is none of your business until she invites you to that information."

After our session, Zack called her and set up a date with her for that night. When I checked my phone while playing basketball at the gym that night, I saw that I had nine missed calls from him in quick succession. It was urgent. Typically, I have set call times with my clients, but I could feel something brewing here. With sweat dripping down my ribs and face, I placed my AirPods in and called him right back. It barely rang one time before he answered.

"Are you okay?" I asked. I made sure my voice expressed a calm frame, as I was anticipating that he would be frantic or full of energy.

"Yes, I'm okay. She's just really into me, and I'm getting nervous," Zack said.

"What are you nervous about?" I asked.

"We just went to dinner. I'm in the bathroom right now, and we are going to go to a lounge after. I just don't want to mess this up!"

"Stop. Speak on what you want. Detach from the outcome you have in your head. I know you have thought about having sex with her again—let it go. I know you want to kiss her under the rain and fall in love again—let the thought go. Be okay with it not happening. Hold the vision of her becoming your girlfriend again in your mind, and then let it go. Be okay with this date being the last. Be okay with her never wanting to see you again. Give yourself the ability to be detached from this, and give everything you have to it. Because these thoughts you keep having are attaching you to anxiety, to overwhelm, and to worry, and that is not the direction we want to create from. You are dealing with the tender spots of soul and love; there is no map for this. There is nothing as a coach I can do other than remind you to be totally present. Love is presence. Allow your soul to be totally present."

He repeated aloud:

*"Detach.*

*Be present.*

*Give my all.*

*Be present.*

*Love is presence."*

He was an echo chamber, and for him, these words brought him a great resonance and calm. I had no idea if this truly was the right thing to say to him. As a coach, you genuinely don't know if what you are saying is "right" because what is right for one may not serve another. There's an attachment you have because you recognize the alchemy in the medicine, and there's a detachment because you truly don't know if it will work. It felt right, in my heart, and that gave me peace.

"Coach, one more line, please," he urged.

"You are worthy of the outcome you seek." That's what I said and then I shut up. That line felt like the perfect staple to this packet of time; it was the closure we both needed. There was silence on the line for about 30 seconds, then we ended the call with an acknowledgment of gratitude toward one another.

After Zack hung up, I said the line to myself, "You are worthy of the outcome you seek." I had to believe in the medicine and words even though I had doubt because of my previous wound. Zack chose to believe in the words, as they were a mirror for what he wanted and needed energetically to get him closer to his dreams, and, somehow, he chose to embrace the possibility of detachment. I went back to playing basketball and he went back to the date.

Since we have the luxury of hindsight with this story, I have the data to share that Zach and his "ex" ended up getting back together. They have three kids together and one home in Denver, Colorado, and one home in Jaco, Costa Rica. They've traveled the world together, supported each other, and have a truly integrated relationship. They were always meant to find each other again, but I think it's even bigger than a poetic line. The ending of their college tenure caused them to detach, to let go, and they both honored that when it was time. Later, they were able to build a foundation that was based in seeing each other raw and real; they were able to be totally in the moment with one another.

### I'm Forcing a Relationship: What Should I Do?

If you find yourself in a similar situation, first, let's invite in a great deal of compassion. And let me set an intention. I am not here to nudge you toward breaking up. I am not here to nudge you toward staying together. My response to this is more along a line of questioning. I could go on and on and tell you what to do, but the answers are within.

If you feel like you are forcing a relationship with someone, I want you to ask yourself these four questions. Now, to be clear, I am using the word *relationship* in general, covering all human relationships. While yes, there are intricate difference among family, friendships, and dating, the essence of these four questions should be deep enough to guide you toward the right actions.

Second, let's not blame the other person or have a victim posture. I challenge you to answer these questions completely in your power and to take full responsibility for your participation. I don't want these questions to push your brain into overperforming, co-dependency, or any people-pleasing type of frame. The purpose of these questions is to recognize a problem, to bring medicine to solving them, and to help you and the other person heal and move forward—if possible.

- Can I stay in this connection as-is without anything changing? If the answer is no, what needs to change and why? If safe, is it possible that you can communicate exactly what you need to heal, repair, and move forward?

- What can you do better in the present moment? What can you bring more of? How can you be better in this situation? Are you giving your highest self to this?

- Is the "problem" a big deal? Some problems are amplified because of past wounds and our stories. In the present, is this problem as big as it has been made out to be?

- Are you direct? Are they direct? You both need to be direct. Most relationship issues happen as an avoidance of the issue, which keeps us further away from resolution. We must commit to being direct. Being direct doesn't mean the message has to be delivered in an unkind way. We can be direct and respectful and still honor one another.

## THE ART OF DETACHMENT IN VOCATION AND CAREER

We talked about the importance of vocation earlier as it is one of the keys of self-mastery. As someone who was lucky enough and skilled enough and who worked hard at the right time, I was able to get enough leverage and energy going toward the vocation that made the most sense for my soul, for my life. I can tell you with certainty that this won't be the easiest path if you are already in a career, if you have self-doubt, if you have fear, and if you have kids. The truth is, all those factors make sense and are normal, but the ask here is that you choose to detach from normal.

*You must choose to be uncommon.*

You cannot have common thoughts and reach greatness. There are aspects of your life that need you to think bigger, bolder, and braver, and that means you may need to let go of your money mindset. You might need to let go of what you think was possible, especially if it was based in fear or self-doubt.

Creating dreams from fear and self-doubt is the worst way to go about it. If you are fresh out of high school, this journey is going to be much easier for you as you have the luxury of time on your side, and for the most part, you are a clean slate. There are a few components that make this process easier, so let's go deep here.

### Embrace Duality

Energetically accept that it has to work out in your favor *but also* be okay if it doesn't. Okay, this is going to confuse the average person because it sounds contradictory. But that's because the average person thinks in wins or losses, black or white, good or bad. When I went all-in on my writing career by leaving my job at Verizon, I told myself over and over, "This will work out; it must. This will work in my favor; it has to."

That was my plan A. There was no plan B. In the back of my head, I knew I would "be okay" if it didn't because I would find something else that sparked my soul, challenged my brain, was fun, and felt like a place I could call home. The duality here is to hold, honor, and embrace your vision, to see it as a plan A with no plan B—but also to be completely in victor posture so that in case it doesn't pan out, you can pivot quicker to another plan A. Some people take a loss and never pivot. To live the life we deserve, we must be committed to what we want, but we also need to pivot if that just won't occur. Failure may be a possibility, but it won't break us.

### Your "Dream" Situation Might Not Be the Next One

This is okay. We are on a journey, and as we take on different jobs and opportunities, we cannot be irresponsible. We must also acknowledge that each opportunity is here to offer us something, to help us grow in one way or another. We need to take care of the kids, the soil underneath us, and our mental and physical health. If you have attachments, there's still a healthy balance you can use. Don't use the excuse that because you have kids you must give up on yourself.

What are you modeling for them? Maybe the steak dinners stop so you can stack money. Maybe the vacations stop so you can invest in what is needed for you to grow this new idea. Maybe Netflix and expensive haircuts stop for a while. Kids don't need extravagant anything. We as parents know this, but for some reason, we convince ourselves that we need to buy everything to earn their love or to show that we care, but that's far from the truth.

I bought my son a $60 remote-controlled car when we went to the mall, and he broke it on day one. That little truck didn't even last a full 24 hours with my son. That same day, I had a package of books arrive from Hay House. He used the cardboard box that the books came in as a tent, as storage for his make-believe pantry, as a spaceship, as a wrestling ring, and as his personal table instead of the huge kitchen table we have.

We all have this type of proof that as long as basic needs are met and there's an abundance of support, love, creativity, and joy, the excuse that you need to buy a bunch of "things" is a false reality. In fact, some of the most powerful language you can use and share within your family is the language of sacrifice. Modeling to your child things like, "I have this dream, and in order for me to get it, I need to give up cookies for the next three months," will literally plant the seed in them that my parent will go for their dreams, regardless of what is, and they will still handle responsibility.

Powerful.

### Embrace Unpredictability

Acknowledge that the path to your ideal vocation may not unfold in a linear or predictable manner. Instead of clinging to a rigid plan, embrace the twists and turns that come your way. Understand that the journey might take unexpected detours, and that's perfectly okay.

By letting go of the need for a perfectly mapped-out career trajectory, you open yourself up to a realm of calm and possibility. There is no need for the "I should be here" language that so many people use. That language has a great deal of shame and judgment laced in. I have a friend who, because he has a master's degree, always says, "Man, Sly, I should be . . ." And he is alluding to the fact that he should be further along because of education. I caution him to be mindful of that language. His education is not what's holding him back; it's being afraid to move out of the state and to let go of a job that pays him less than he deserves. He is smart, but his energy is not big enough; it's not bold enough yet. Once he realizes that it's energetically time to sit in some new shoes, then he will make more. He will be in alignment with where he thinks he "should" be. He must detach from the "should" so he can go within and work on his self-mastery.

Detaching from the notion of a fixed path allows you to navigate the unpredictable terrain of your career with resilience and adaptability, ultimately leading you to a vocation that aligns authentically with your soul and purpose. I believe with all my heart that each job we take sharpens our skills in life, there is something to learn from each position, and each opportunity can help us in our path toward self-mastery.

## IDENTITY SHIFT

I have a client who is a working actor in Hollywood. You most likely have seen his work at some point or another. As an actor, Jordan has done well for himself and has a legacy that is worth being admired. Now, he doesn't always see it that way, as he is human and has fears, doubts, shame, guilt, and all the emotions that we as humans experience. He sent me an e-mail to let me know that he wasn't doing well; he was feeling underwater and like he couldn't breathe. We agreed to adjust our meeting time so he could get some energy from me.

As we entered our call and started to dive into the day's topic, the story unfolded. Jordan said that he was feeling an immense amount of guilt by keeping employees on his staff that weren't needed anymore. He felt heavy as he was paying for luxurious things for his kids that he wasn't sure they truly valued. In his business, the expenses had reached a point where they outweighed the income. The stress now outweighed the joy.

"You need to make a change here. So let's start with the emotional side first, and then move to strategy. We need to be aware of the consciousness we are creating from before we can discuss strategy. Tell me exactly how you are feeling and what's going on," I said in a safe, hand-holding voice as we co-created a safe vessel for him to unveil what he was feeling.

He sighed.

He took a deep breath in and out.

Then, he was ready to speak.

"Sylvester, I feel dumb. Nobody knows this besides you, but I put myself in credit card debt. I haven't had debt since my twenties, and here I am. I feel like I'm keeping on certain staff members because they gave up their dreams to work for me, and I am paying them well. But the work they do and the income right now just doesn't seem to make sense. I want people to like me. I want people to love me. I want you to like me. We just took the kids on a trip, and I couldn't even continue. I haven't paid myself at all this year from the business, and last year we were thriving because there was so much money coming in."

I jumped in as soon as he finished talking. "Okay, let's name the thing where you are saying you just want people to like you. You want people to love you. You're an adult and a business owner, and while those feelings are certainly valid on a human level, to make the decisions that are going to keep your business alive and afloat, you'll need to detach from those desires and find new ones that propel you.

"You're naming that you want to be a successful business owner, feel lighter, and not have this guilt. The only way to do that is to reframe how you are looking at this. You must reframe the identity. The kid in you wants to be liked, sure. The adult in you needs to realize that you are being inauthentic by chasing approval and chasing these people to like you. Your business is suffering because you are letting the desires of the child be the most dominant ones. That ends today, unless you want to continue to suffer, and I don't think you do. Before we get to the strategy of how to do that, tell me a little bit more about the credit card debt."

He responded, "See, when I had this show running last year, I was making a lot of money, and I lived a certain lifestyle. Well, when that show ended, I kept the same lifestyle and even started spending more and doing more. I thought the money would come back, and there would be another show right away, but that hasn't been the case. I have this big hole, and the more I fight the hole, the more I become the hole."

I jumped back in. "Okay, so you said nobody knows about this credit card debt—what about your partner?"

He said, "Nobody knows about it."

"Understood. Step one, sir, is you must confront this entire situation. This is a predator, and you must do the great work of attacking it. You're hiding due to shame, but we need to get the help and support you deserve. You must come out from behind that little kid and know that you are strong enough as an adult to manage this. You have to confront these hard conversations.

"The first thing I want you to do is tell your partner about the debt. I know there's fear, shame, and guilt. You feel like a failure, but you must seek support. You must say exactly what level of support you need. If your partner doesn't know that things have changed, they won't be able to support you in the change. They'll just assume the money is as it was. Your identity as a business owner has changed. Last year, you were earning an out-of-this-world amount of money, and it enabled you to live freely without a budget, without care, but that's not the identity this year. This year, you need to be sharp, focused, and on point, and you can't get there if you hide this conversation from your partner.

"Now, as far as strategy goes there, you can use the snowball method of credit card repayment. You pay off all the minimum payments on everything you owe, and then throw everything you can at the smallest balance. Then, after you wipe that balance out, you direct all your extra funds to the next smallest. You repeat this process until you have completed it.

"Once you embrace these emotions and the story with them, you see that the strategy and execution of the strategy is easy. Does this make sense?"

Jordan sighed. "Yes, I'm starting to feel lighter. Can we go back to my assistant, social media manager, and other team members? The amount I'm paying them just feels like a massive hemorrhage, and it's draining me. I'm not sure how to attack that."

"You read my book, *Care Package*?" I asked.

"Yes, I read that book. I go back to it often."

I continued, "Good. Well, the first step to healing a wound is to acknowledge it. You just said that it feels like a hemorrhage, which is an open wound. You are acknowledging the wound. In the first chapter of *Care Package*, I wrote about alignment and how alignment is the first step of healing. As you look to repair your business, you must understand that this is all about alignment. *Repair* means to heal. We don't often think of business or vocation in this way, but this is the great work that you must do. You must repair what is.

"So here's the data: you have these roles in your business, you pay them a lot of money—even above market rate—and you as a business owner do not feel like the work they create or the amount of work is in alignment with what you pay. Therefore, you only have three options. One: you get rid of them. Two: you ask them to do more work so they can justify what you are paying. Three: you do a reduction in hours and workload to keep them on but make the costs more manageable.

"The guilt you have is normal because you feel bad if you have to release someone. You don't want to hurt anyone, but that is not what you are doing. You are looking at data, being honest, and most importantly as a leader of this business, you are being authentic. This business was thriving when you were real with yourself about where you were. As you allowed these emotions to go untouched and unseen, the business went south. I know that you are a heart-centered person and that's why you feel guilty, but you must detach from that for this assignment. The great work here is to confront the data and have a real conversation with yourself about what you want.

"Do not, I repeat, do not make a decision based on co-dependency or people-pleasing. It doesn't matter if we like you. What matters is that you are authentic and that you like you. As you move more toward embodying your truth, you'll move away from this childlike desire to be liked. Whatever decisions you make need to be based in keeping your business alive, and they need to be decisions that give you the ability to feel lighter and drive revenue."

He took a minute or so to gather himself, then said, "I get what you are doing, and I see where you are sending me. You are making me detach from this kid in me. You are making me detach from the old me who was making a certain amount. You are making me live in this reality. I have been hiding this conversation from my partner about credit card debt out of fear, because of shame, and you are making me talk about it because that is how I will repair it.

My entire identity has changed, and I haven't caught up, and that's why I am suffering now."

I jumped back in. "Yes, you have been so attached to the emotions that it clouded your ability to make sound decisions. Now that we have moved to and through the emotions, it's easier to make decisions now. Our identities define us; they also have the ability be jail cells if we don't recognize what we are being attached to. As you became attached to a particular lifestyle, you didn't give yourself the vision to see when things pivoted externally thus you didn't and now you are suffering. But now that we talked, you have a way out, and I want you to be mindful of the visions of yourself that you have and the identities that you attach yourself to in the future. I hope that moving forward, you can be detached from that kid in you when making these big decisions. I would rather you live an authentic life, one that is based on the data of what is and be okay with who likes you based on your authenticity rather than who likes you when you are being phony and fake to yourself. Does this resonate?"

He heaved a massive sigh and said, "I can finally breathe again. This is everything I needed. I was afraid to talk to you because I thought you might wag your finger at me. That was my own projection. You held my hand as we crossed this street, and now I am safe. Now I am on the other side. Now I see a way out. I'm ready to embrace this great work. I'm ready to let go of who I was and what I was so I can fully embody who I am today. Thank you."

## DISCONNECT FROM SOCIETY, NEWS CYCLES, AND SOCIAL MEDIA: GENUINELY CONNECT TO YOUR COMMUNITY

We are not supposed to know this many people. We are not supposed to know this much information about people. Our brains do not need to know about celebrities and news from places we've never been. We will thrive more when we bring our brains back into a community, back into keeping up with a smaller group of folks. We will thrive more when we focus on genuine connections in person, via touch and technology that allows us to engage in conversation where we can see, hear, and feel one another's energy.

The pendulum is swinging, and it's time for us to go backward until we find a place that makes sense to our soul. We have gone too far. Those of us who want to thrive in all pillars of life must focus on developing healthy connections, taking our time, and valuing who is right in front of us. I want to be clear that I am not vilifying social media or any news outlet. I just feel like our society relies on social media too much, on the news too much, on the external too much. We all know someone, and we may even be that person, that if we would just go within, we could fix certain situations, and it would change our lives. We know people who are obsessed with the exterior. They can tell you everything about a certain celebrity of sports star. I'm not shaming it. I'm just asking you, me, and anyone who can see this page to reel it in, make sure we are focusing on our wellness, and have boundaries with how much information and energy we take in.

*This society benefits if you hate yourself.*

The goal of highly controlled mass media is to set you up and keep you trapped in the loop of "I am unworthy."

As long as we agree to this co-creation, they win their little game, and we are pawns who are being moved and pitted against each other. We are buying into their division.

Why?

Money.

Why?

Mind control.

Are you ready to break that loop forever and reclaim the power that is inside you? Are you ready to tap into the art of deliberate creation? Are you ready to shed years of identity so you can stand inside your truth worth, your human worth? This great work will require you to fight. This great work will require you to face predators. This great work will require you to grieve, let go, and open your heart to abundance. Are you ready for war? I am, and as your general, I am going to fight alongside you. We will overcome everything that is meant to destroy us.

*We deserve to live the life we want.*

*We deserve to be rich in experience, in soul, in connection.*

*We deserve to feel the wealth of joy and the breeze of peace of mind as it flows over our skin like a calm fall wind.*

Capitalism is the fabric of this modern society, and that is why many of us are suffering invisible battles. Our brains are not meant to process this many ads, this many commercials, this much advice and ideas. Our brains thrive when we know 75 to 100 people max at varying levels. We must bring our brains back into a community, back into keeping up with a smaller group of folks, in order to thrive.

According to British anthropologist Robin Dunbar, the "magic number" for the size of one's social circle is 150. Dunbar became convinced that there was a ratio between brain sizes and group sizes through his studies of nonhuman primates. This ratio was mapped out using neuroimaging and observation of time spent on grooming, an important social behavior of primates. Dunbar concluded that the size of the neocortex—the part of the brain associated with cognition and language—relative to the body is linked to the size of a cohesive social group. This ratio limits how much complexity a social system can handle.[5]

I don't believe that we should accept this blindly and lock our brain onto this. Life changes. Capacity changes. Desires and needs change. When I was in high school, I was a star football player and knew thousands of people. I hung out with hundreds of people often, and that was fine. When I first started my writing career, I had my girlfriend, a few friends, and hardly anyone else. As I write to you now, I have a big family, maybe six to eight close friends, and hundreds of acquaintances that are in my phone, some of whom I've never even met other than in conversations on social media. In your life, I'm sure you have seen similar changes as well.

Overall, I think the key word is *capacity*. Personally, I do not have the capacity inside my soul or the energy to emotionally process what is happening across the world. There is both great news and bad news everywhere. I can't cry and be upset at every injustice or tragedy; it's unfair to put that pressure on myself. I can hold space, support, and feel whatever appropriate emotion when someone in my network is going through it. And let's not assume it's all darkness. Right now, someone just reached their dreams of becoming an author. Since I don't know them in this present moment, I wouldn't feel much if I saw that as a headline. However, let's say it was you. You're in my network. You're one of my people. I would jump for joy when your e-mail landed on me. I most likely would say some-thing like, "Yes, I'm proud of you. When does the book come out and what inspired you to write it?" I would have more capacity for it. This applies to you as well. Let me stay in this pocket but switch gears for one second.

If you've followed me on social media, you may notice that I do not post about current events, news, or anything tragic that happens in the world. The way I am going to explain this is extremely important, and I think it can serve a lot of people. For me, social media has a specific purpose, and I have clear and detailed boundaries for it. I use it to share my work. This is my work. I am not a reporter or someone who gives an opinion on current events publicly; however, I am human and present just like you. When those world events come up, for me, I want to see them as sacred, and I want to bring them to my com-munity. I want to talk about the nuances and details with people who know how to hold space, with people who have empathy, with people who care to listen and learn. I refuse to waste my energy engaging with people who want to scream or argue and truly only care about other people being forced into agreement with their perspec-tive—we all know the type. Why? Because that type of energy is not for me. There are some people who love to argue. Their platform is to debate—is that you? Probably not, and it's certainly not me. Give yourself permission to choose what is best for you. If you are into politics, that's fine—but don't make others be into it. If you are into to talking about current events that are deep, dramatic, and heavy, cool—just don't think you must force everyone into that. If you are indifferent and couldn't care less, then honor what is present and authentic for you. If you do not know enough to have an opinion, that is okay, and you're allowed to sit back and learn.

We do not have to fit into these boxes and molds; that's all a part of the mind control game. In life, we all change and evolve. Who knows? Maybe in 10 years I may only speak about current events since I will be an elder in the community, and maybe my leadership on said things will be required—that's possible.

# JOURNAL PROMPTS:
# DETACHMENT AND CONNECTION

- Think about a situation in your life with an uncertain outcome. Describe different possible ways that things may turn out. Practice detachment as you write, not feeling drawn to any particular result.

- Write down all the relationships within your family, friends, and community that you find valuable. Estimate how long you spend nurturing each connection. Then write down all the different media you interact with throughout your day, including news, radio, podcasts, sports, and social media. Estimate how long you spend with each one. Is there an imbalance with how you're allocating your time?

- Describe how the different media you interact with makes you *feel* and what you get out of the relationship. Does any of it serve your goals?

- Describe what your life would look like if you detached from the pressure of society, news, and social media.

If you watch the news and scroll through social media every day, you will have unnecessary extra stress and anxiety. One of the best ways to release energy, to hear your own thoughts, and to live a happier life is to set boundaries with social media and the news. When you use these tools, have a purpose and clear-cut reason for using them. Boredom is not a good reason. If you're bored, go for a walk, take a nap, or write a love letter. There are better ways to use your time. Your boundaries will help you thrive.

— **Sylvester McNutt III,** *Live the Life You Deserve*

Reconnect to your journey and to what makes you unique. Let go of the desire to check what the world is doing and check on your world. Your world needs you to be present and to show up. There will always be a time to get on the phone and see what others are doing, but you need you right now. Focus on you.

— **Sylvester McNutt III,** *Live the Life You Deserve*

Reconnect to nature and getting outside more. Reconnect to the air outside and go for long walks. We are not meant to be hunched over screens and computers at the rate we are doing so. Free yourself and get outside more. You deserve all the benefits that come from more intentional time in nature.

— **Sylvester McNutt III**, *Live the Life You Deserve*

This is your message from the universe to stop forcing what you are forcing. Think about the energy of forcing and what it looks like. If you walked in on a mechanic fixing your car and you saw him banging and clanging something that didn't fit into a space it was designed for, you would not drive that car, would you? Some things are natural fits. Don't force yourself to be aligned with an identity that is not you. Fall in love with the concept of flowing more. Jobs, relationships, and your overall wellness will improve more when you flow. Fall in love with the version of you who knows when to flow and knows when to apply pressure.

— **Sylvester McNutt III**, *Live the Life You Deserve*

# CHAPTER 11

# IT'S POSSIBLE

You've done the work. You have shown up. You have survived, and you have fought to be where you are. You've shed tears that some people may not understand, and you've helped people along the way. Now, it's your time and it's your turn—and you deserve it. It's your turn to get the love you keep giving away. It's your time to be nourished, loved, and respected. It's your time to step though the bad habits that may be holding you back.

Everything you need is inside you. My hope is that if you feel you lack anything, *Live the Life You Deserve* brought you into or prepared you for the invitation that will get you what you need. Life is fragile, and every day we have is important. You matter, and the way you show up in other people's lives matter.

As you prepare to close this book, just know it's possible. You *can* live the life you deserve. Know that the journey still goes on. So here are my three asks of you.

- *Write a letter:* I want you to write a letter to future you. It will help with integrating the lessons from this book. I want you to write down your biggest commitment moving forward and the future you can expect in the present moment.

- *Tell someone you love them:* You might do this every day. You might be one of those people who avoids using this word at all costs. No matter who you are, we all need love. We need to feel love, and we need to give love. That is one of the common denominators of human experience. Take time today to genuinely tell someone you love them. Create a home for everything that you deserve.

- *Repeat that it's possible:* You chose this book and these words because you had a question about possibility, and you knew that this book would give you a spark, insight, or energy that would guide you to where you needed to land.

I will now leave you with more writings under the theme of expansion and possibility. Tattoo them. Journal them. Scream them. Share them. Read them to your yoga class. Read them to your students. Read them before bed.

*Live the Life You Deserve* is all about what's possible and the expansion of our inner energy.

I love you. Thank you for reading, and I hope you go *live the life you deserve.*

What you want is a powerful attracter of energy. Choose what you want. This is your life. Choose the college you want. Choose the partner you want. Choose the career that brings something out of you. Do not just go through the motions with anything. Choose what you truly want because life is the reflection of how you will listen to and manage your desires.

— **Sylvester McNutt III,** *Live the Life You Deserve*

No matter what you want to create or who you want to be, you must hold an unequivocal belief that it is possible. This is your sign from the universe that you can and should fall in love with the realm of possibility for your life. Yes, stay grounded in reality, but increase your concept of reality. You have greatness in you, and it's your duty to tap in, to believe in yourself, and to remember that it's possible.

— **Sylvester McNutt III,** *Live the Life You Deserve*

I consider myself lucky.
I believe in the law of attraction, in the law that I am deliberately creating my experience. If luck is a thing, then I believe am lucky and that luck will benefit me. I am calling in all the luck and the great blessings it will bring.

— **Sylvester McNutt III,** *Live the Life You Deserve*

Don't believe that everything is solely about hard work—there are elements of luck with everything. I believe we can create more luck though by being in the right place at the right time with the right mindset. Some of the luck that we have is just because we showed up.

— **Sylvester McNutt III,** *Live the Life You Deserve*

If you ever feel stuck between two choices, ask yourself this question: What do I want to experience? One of the answers will tell you what to do next. Sometimes, getting what you deserve is about asking yourself the right questions, which will lead you to an aligned action.

— **Sylvester McNutt III,** *Live the Life You Deserve*

There's always something you have to give up to get something new that you want. Sacrifice is the only way to transform your life, to live the life you deserve. You must give something up. What is it?

— **Sylvester McNutt III,** *Live the Life You Deserve*

S acrifice what you need to sacrifice so you can move in the direction that is in alignment with your journey. Let go of what was so you can use your magnetic energy and the law of attraction to call forth and to live in alignment with what will come. It won't be easy, but there will be a natural order and flow to this process. At first, it may feel clunky since this is new, but trust the process. Trust that you are rewiring your brain for greatness and for pockets of authenticity.

— **Sylvester McNutt III,** *Live the Life You Deserve*

A s the designer of your life, give yourself permission to laugh off and laugh at things that are beneath you. Release the child's play like pettiness and revenge; focus on your mission and path.

— **Sylvester McNutt III,** *Live the Life You Deserve*

If you would ever have a conversation with me in real life and we talk about your goals, I would listen deeply. The first thing I would tell you to do is to be specific. Ninety-nine percent of people I listen to are not specific enough when they talk about their goals, desires, and dreams. And the second thing I would tell you to do is to go ahead and start the process of sacrificing something. I don't say that to put you in hustle mode. I say that to alert your consciousness. You want something different than what you have, and you have to give up something you do have to make space—it's time to let go.

— **Sylvester McNutt III,** *Live the Life You Deserve*

Anything is possible if you get your energy right, use the emotion of love, and release what no longer serves you. We cannot waste any more years holding on to what is no longer serving us. It is time to let go so you can live in your highest vibration, so you can live as your highest self. Anything is possible when it comes to your dreams and your possibilities. Believe in what you can do and be curious about what you cannot. Speak love and powerful words into your journey and into how you will approach things. Laugh more and allow yourself to experience true joy and fun. You are allowed to have fun, to enjoy this beautiful life, and to have a reverence and deep appreciation for your life. I hope you take time today to be proud of your journey and to take one more step forward in the direction that is calling you next. You are worthy. You are love. You matter. You are important and I love you.

Go live the life you deserve.

— **Sylvester McNutt III**, *Live the Life You Deserve*

# ENDNOTES

## Chapter 1

1. Counselling Pastoral Trust. "List of Schemas." www
   .counsellingpastoraltrust.org/list-of-schemas.

2. Ibid.

## Chapter 2

1. Encyclopedia Brittanica. "Brahmacharya Buddhism." www
   .britannica.com/topic/brahmacharya.

2. Oppezzo, Marily and Daniel Schwartz. "Give Your Ideas Some Legs:
   The Positive Effect of Walking on Creative Thinking." *Journal of
   Experimental Psychology: Learning, Memory, and Cognition* 40, no. 4,
   1142–1152. www.apa.org/pubs/journals/releases/xlm-a0036577.pdf.

3. Bryant, Kobe. 2018. *The Mamba Mentality*. New York: MCD, p. 69.

## Chapter 3

1. Jung, Carl, and William McGuire. *Dream Analysis: Notes of the Seminar
   Given in 1928–30*. Princeton, NJ: Princeton University Press, 1983.

2. Weller, Francis. *Alchemy of Initiation*. Audio program, Francis Weller,
   2019. https://www.francisweller.net/the-alchemy-of-initiation-a
   -five-week-series.html.

3. Ibid.

## Chapter 5

1. Mehrtens, Sue. "Jung on Perfection and Completeness." Jungian
   Center for the Spiritual Sciences. August 30, 2021. https://
   jungiancenter.org/jung-on-perfection-and-completeness/#_ftn38.

2. Brown, Brené. *The Gifts of Imperfection: Let Go of Who You Think You're
   Supposed to Be and Embrace Who You Are*. Center City, MN: Hazelden,
   2014.

3. Kumai, Candice. *Kintsugi Wellness*. New York: HarperCollins, 2018.

4. Vasarhelyi, Elizabeth Chai and Jimmy Chin, dirs. *Free Solo*. Washington, DC: National Geographic Documentary Film, 2018.

5. Bryant, Kobe. "TEDxShanghaiSalon, Power of the Mind." June 28, 2016. YouTube. www.youtube.com/watch?v=9_tYXFbgjZk.

6. Learn with Jaspal. "I ENJOY WORKING HARD | TOM CRUISE." May 17, 2023. YouTube. https://www.youtube.com/watch?v=OEoj09Iyw0I

7. Washington, Denzel. "Fall Forward: Denzel Washington's Inspiring Commencement Speeches." www.characteractionmedia.com/wp-content/uploads/2019/06/D-Washington-Speech-Transcript.pdf.

8. Greene, Robert. *Mastery*. New York: Penguin Books, 2013.

9. Ibid.

10. Merriam-Webster.com Dictionary. "Vocation." https://www.merriam-webster.com/dictionary/vocation.

## Chapter 6

1. Hicks, Esther and Jerry. *The Law of Attraction*. Carlsbad, CA: Hay House, 2006.

2. Ibid.

3. Ibid.

4. Ibid.

5. Ibid.

6. Dispenza, Joe. *Breaking the Habit of Being Yourself: How to Lose Your Mind and Create a New One*. Carlsbad, CA: Hay House, 2016.

## Chapter 7

1. Kübler-Ross, Elisabeth. *On Death and Dying*. New York: Macmillan, 1969.

2. Ho, Judy. "5 Stages of Grief (It's NOT Depression)." YouTube. www.youtube.com/watch?v=ZNv_mK6FGCE.

3. Weller, Francis. *Entering the Healing Ground: Grief, Ritual and the Soul of the World*. Berkeley, CA: North Atlantic Books, 2015.

4. Weller, Francis. *The Wild Edge of Sorrow: Rituals of Renewal and the Sacred Work of Grief*. Berkeley, CA: North Atlantic Books, 2015.

5. Moffa, Gina. *Moving on Doesn't Mean Letting Go: A Modern Guide to Navigating Loss*. New York: Balance, 2023.

6. Ibid.

## Chapter 8

1. McNutt, Sylvester. "Repetition Rewires the Brain with Dr. Jen Wolkin." *Free Your Energy*. Podcast audio, January 2, 2023.

2. American Psychological Association. APA Dictionary of Psychology. "Joy." https://dictionary.apa.org/joy.

3. Brittle, Zach. "Turn Towards Instead of Away." The Gottman Institute. https://www.gottman.com/blog/turn-toward-instead-of-away.

4. Watts, Alan. "Work as Play." *The Essence of Alan Watts*. Millbrae, CA: Celestial Arts, 1977.

5. Ibid.

## Chapter 9

1. Merriam-Webster.com Dictionary. "Ritual." www.merriam-webster.com/dictionary/ritual.

2. Merriam-Webster.com Dictionary. "Routine." www.merriam-webster.com/dictionary/routine.

3. Duhigg, Charles. *The Power of Habit: Why We Do What We Do in Life and Business.* New York: Random House, 2014.

## Chapter 10

1. Bowlby, John. *Attachment: Attachment and Loss.* New York: Basic Books, 1983.

2. Simpson, Jeffry, and Steven Rholes. "Adult Attachment, Stress, and Romantic Relationships." *Current Opinion in Psychology* 13, no. 13 (February 2017): 19–24. www.ncbi.nlm.nih.gov/pmc/articles/PMC4845754.

3. Brown, Ryan. "Made of Honor." *Hidden Brain*. Podcast audio, March 20, 2023. https://hiddenbrain.org/podcast/made-of-honor.

4. McNutt, Sylvester. "Integrated Principles of Masculinity | Traver Boehm." *Free Your Energy*. Podcast audio, October 3, 2022. https://www.sylvestermcnutt.net/recent-episodes/2022/10/3/integrated-principles-of-masculinity-with-traver-boehm.

5. "Dunbar's Number: Why We Can Only Maintain 150 Relationships." October 9, 2019. www.bbc.com/future/article/20191001-dunbars-number-why-we-can-only-maintain-150-relationships.

# ACKNOWLEDGMENTS

I feel a great deal of joy and love for so many people throughout life and during the writing process of this book. I am thankful for the support of everyone who has helped me write, coach, teach, lead, and do all the things I am able to do.

Special thanks to Jan and Steve, my agents, for their hard work, communication, and support. My gratitude to Mark, Branden, Juan, Will, Colin, Ted, Carla, Jen, Jeremy, Chris, Dan, James, to all of my dear coaching clients, to the people who have paid to hear me speak, and to anyone who follows this work on social media.

I'm so appreciative of my family and friends for being in my corner. A special thank you to Mason for being my relentless son who is full of love and energy. To Daisy for being the best mother he could ask for and an even better partner for me. To my father, Sylvester, and mother, Delcynthia, for putting journals, books, and encyclopedias in my room when I was younger. For pushing me, teaching me, and guiding me to pursue excellence.

Finally, I honor my journey of being an author for over 10 years. It has been worth it, and I'm excited to see how this book impacts its readers.

To all of you: Thank you for reading. Without you, this work would be meaningless.

With love and compassion,
*Sylvester*

# ABOUT THE AUTHOR

**Sylvester McNutt III** is a best-selling author, podcaster, public speaker, course creator, and father. He teaches people how to transform their mindsets through self-awareness and healing practices. As a retired arena football player and survivor of traumatic experiences, he has used storytelling to teach people how to introspect, gain confidence, and sustain self-love. Sylvester's core belief is that healing is the key to success and self-awareness unlocks freedom. Sylvester's passions are writing, lifting, traveling, yoga, and exploring the human existence.

*Website:* **www.sylvestermcnutt.net**

# Hay House Titles of Related Interest

We hope you enjoyed this Hay House book. If you'd like to receive our online catalog featuring additional information on Hay House books and products, or if you'd like to find out more about the Hay Foundation, please contact:

Hay House LLC, P.O. Box 5100, Carlsbad, CA 92018-5100
(760) 431-7695 or (800) 654-5126
www.hayhouse.com® • www.hayfoundation.org

———

***Published in Australia by:***
Hay House Australia Publishing Pty Ltd
18/36 Ralph St., Alexandria NSW 2015
*Phone:* +61 (02) 9669 4299
www.hayhouse.com.au

***Published in the United Kingdom by:***
Hay House UK Ltd
The Sixth Floor, Watson House,
54 Baker Street, London W1U 7BU
*Phone:* +44 (0) 203 927 7290
www.hayhouse.co.uk

***Published in India by:***
Hay House Publishers (India) Pvt Ltd
Muskaan Complex, Plot No. 3,
B-2, Vasant Kunj, New Delhi 110 070
*Phone:* +91 11 41761620
www.hayhouse.co.in

———

## Let Your Soul Grow

Experience life-changing transformation—one video at a time—with guidance from the world's leading experts.

www.healyourlifeplus.com